A Place to Start

A NEW BELIEVER'S GUIDE TO MEETING GOD AS AN ADULT

JESSICA EICH

Paperback: 978-1-969816-09-3
Hardcover: 978-1-969816-08-6
Ebook: 978-1-969816-10-9

Printed in the United States of America.

TABLE OF CONTENTS

INTRODUCTION

Starting a faith journey as an adult can feel overwhelming. Many resources assume you already know the language, the stories, or the structure of church life. This workbook was created for those who do not.

A Place to Start is a guided workbook designed to help adults who are new to faith or newly curious about God begin exploring what belief looks like in a practical, honest, and approachable way. You do not need prior knowledge, church experience, or a polished faith to begin.

Throughout this workbook, you will be introduced to foundational aspects of Christian faith, including who God is, how to read and understand the Bible, prayer, and what it means to grow in relationship with God over time. Each section includes simple explanations, Scripture, and space to reflect and respond.

This is not a workbook meant to be rushed or completed all at once. It is designed to be used slowly and intentionally. You will be invited to write, pause, question, and return to ideas as your understanding grows. There is no right pace and no expectation of perfection.

The pages ahead are designed to help you begin your journey meeting God.

A NOTE FROM JESS

Hi there,

If you're holding this book, it means something important is happening in your life. Whether you're curious about God, have recently started believing, or are still unsure what faith even looks like, I want to tell you:

You're not too late. You're not behind. You're not the only one.

This workbook is for adults who didn't grow up in church. It's for people who've walked through life with questions, hurts, and doubts and are now learning that there is a God who deeply loves them.

In these pages, I hope you'll find explanations, room to wrestle, space to reflect, and reminders of who God is and how near He can be.

There is no wrong way to go through this. You can write, cry, question, skip pages, or come back to them later. This is your space, your journey.

I'm so glad you're here.

MY STORY

I didn't grow up in church. I didn't know the Bible stories everyone else seemed to know. I started this faith journey at age 37—not as a lifelong believer but as someone stepping in with a ton of questions, very little knowledge, and a heart that was somehow both terrified and completely on fire.

I felt it all. The confusion, frustration, and fear of getting it wrong. I was passionate to know more, yet angry that I couldn't understand what I wanted so badly to understand. I did my best to juggle the peace, tears, love, doubt, guilt, and hope.

I searched everywhere for educational resources made for someone like me: an adult with a real past and no faith background to build on. I found plenty of resources for kids, teens, or those with years of church language under their belt, but I couldn't find an interactive workbook for adults.

I wanted a space to process what I was feeling and also pointed me to truth. I needed a place to ask what felt like "dumb questions" (spoiler: they're not dumb)—a spot to write, cry, reflect, and learn without pressure to perform or pretend.

I needed a guide that was part creative outlet, part study tool, and part "companion for the chaos" as I figured out what this whole journey with God really meant. So, I made this.

I'm still learning, growing, and figuring things out one step at a time. But I'm at a place now where I want to help others who are just getting started, people who feel exactly how I once did.

If that's you, I hope this workbook becomes a safe, steady, and encouraging place for you. You're not alone, and you're absolutely not disqualified.

You are right on time.

MY PLACE TO START

Before moving forward, take a moment to reflect on where you are right now. This is your starting point. Write honestly about what you believe, what you are unsure of, and what led you here.

There is no pressure to have the right words. This is simply a snapshot of where your heart is at the beginning of this journey.

You will return to this page at the end of the workbook. When you read it again, you may notice ways your thoughts, questions, and understanding have grown.

Some prompts to get you started:

- Why did I pick up this workbook?
- What do I believe about God right now?
- What am I scared of?
- What am I hoping will change?
- What questions are sitting heavy on my heart?
- What do I want to remember about this beginning?

____

____

____

____

____

____

____

____

BEFORE YOU BEGIN

This isn't a devotional or a Bible study; it's a starting place.

Each short chapter focuses on ideas tied to topics like prayer, Scripture, worship, and community. In each chapter, you'll find a few Take a Moment sections to pause and reflect right before journaling prompts and a Final Thoughts section that you carry into the next chapter.

In the back of the book, you'll find a glossary with simple definitions of church terms or phrases you might not be familiar with. There is also space for journaling—a place to write down prayers, questions, sermon notes, or anything God is showing you along the way.

This workbook is designed to be a guide, not a finish line. The goal isn't to give you every answer, but to help you discover what you believe, what you're learning, and what questions you still have. As you move through these pages, you may find areas where you want to dig deeper. When that happens, consider talking with a pastor, a trusted friend, or someone in your church community who can walk alongside you.

There is no right or wrong way to use this. Go in order or skip around and come back to chapters as often as you need. Just start where you are, and God will meet you.

CHAPTER ONE

WHO IS THIS GOD WE SEEK?

GOD THE FATHER, JESUS THE SON, AND THE HOLY SPIRIT

Before we talk about the Bible, the church, or even what it means to be saved, we need to get familiar with who we're really talking about.

This chapter isn't a theology textbook. It isn't meant to explain every mystery or debate every doctrine. This is a starting point—a place to learn the basics of who God, Jesus, and the Holy Spirit are.

You don't have to be an expert or need to have grown up in church. This chapter is for you: the one who's just beginning, has questions, and may feel unqualified, unsure, or overwhelmed. You're in the right place.

We're going to walk slowly through the way Christians understand God as one in three persons.

- God the Father
- Jesus the Son
- The Holy Spirit

This is called the **Trinity**. That word doesn't appear in the Bible, but the idea is there from beginning to end. It might sound confusing (even long-time believers wrestle with understanding it), but don't stress.

This chapter isn't about having perfect answers; it's about getting to know who God is, what He's like, and what kind of relationship He wants with you.

You don't have to have your life cleaned up or your questions figured out yet. Just start here and stay open.

GOD THE FATHER

God is the creator of everything: the sky, earth, stars, and every living thing. He made the whole world on purpose for a purpose, including you. He knows you better than anyone else and cares about every detail of your life. God is holy, which means He is perfect and pure, but He is also loving and close. Even though God is powerful and above all things, He wants to have a close relationship with you. He wants to be your loving Father and friend. He wants to be someone you can trust, talk to, and rely on every day. No matter where you are or what you've been through, God welcomes you with open arms and is ready to walk with you on this new journey.

WHO HE IS

- **Creator of Everything**

  In the beginning God created the heavens and the earth. (Genesis 1:1)

- **Holy and Just**

  The Lord is righteous in all his ways and faithful in all he does. (Psalm 145:17)

- **Merciful and Full of Love**

  The Lord is compassionate and gracious, slow to anger, abounding in love. (Psalm 103:8)

- **A Perfect Father (even if your earthly one isn't)**

  See what great love the Father has lavished on us, that we should be called children of God! (1 John 3:1)

- **Personal, Present, and Not Afraid of Your Doubts or Fears**

  The Lord is near to all who call on him. (Psalm 145:18)

- **Faithful and Trustworthy (He keeps His promises)**

  Know therefore that the Lord your God is God; he is the faithful God, keeping his covenant of love to a thousand generations. (Deuteronomy 7:9)

- **A Refuge and Source of Strength in Hard Times**

  God is our refuge and strength, an ever-present help in trouble. (Psalm 46:1)

WHAT HE HAS DONE FOR US

- **Gave Us Life and Breath**

  The Lord God formed man from the dust of the ground and breathed into his nostrils the breath of life. (Genesis 2:7)

- **Pursues Relationship with His People**

  I will walk among you and be your God, and you will be my people. (Leviticus 26:12)

- **Sent Jesus to Rescue Us from Sin and Separation**

  For God so loved the world that He gave His one and only Son. (John 3:16)

- **Faithfully Keeps His Promises to His People**

  The Lord is trustworthy in all he promises and faithful in all he does. (Psalm 145:13)

- **Loves Us Unconditionally (even when we don't deserve it)**

  But God demonstrates his own love for us in this: While we were still sinners, Christ died for us. (Romans 5:8)

- **Offers Forgiveness to Anyone Who Turns to Him**

  If we confess our sins, He is faithful and just and will forgive us our sins. (1 John 1:9)

- **Gives Us the Holy Spirit (to guide and comfort us)**

  And I will ask the Father, and He will give you another Advocate to help you and be with you forever. (John 14:16)

- **Provides Peace That Goes Beyond Understanding**

  And the peace of God, which transcends all understanding, will guard your hearts and your minds in Christ Jesus. (Philippians 4:7)

- **Hears Our Prayers and Cares Deeply for Us**

  The Lord is close to the brokenhearted and saves those who are crushed in spirit. (Psalm 34:18)

- **Gives Strength When We Feel Weak**

  He gives strength to the weary and increases the power of the weak. (Isaiah 40:29)

THE NAMES OF GOD

When we think of God, we often use just one name: God. Yet Scripture shows us that He reveals Himself through many names—each one offering a glimpse into His character, power, and relationship with us. God's names are not just titles; they are personal, relational, and deeply meaningful. They help us understand who He is and who He promises to be for us.

WHY DOES HE HAVE SO MANY NAMES?

Throughout the Bible, God's people encountered Him in different ways. Sometimes He provided. Sometimes He healed. Sometimes He saw them in their pain, fought for them, or gave them peace. Each encounter revealed a new layer of His identity, often followed by a name that matched the moment.

Knowing the names of God allows us to call on Him specifically. When we are in need, hurting, or praising Him, we can speak to the very part of His character meeting us in that moment.

Yahweh (YHWH): "I AM WHO I AM"

Yahweh is one of the most sacred and significant names for God in the Bible. It's the name God used when He revealed Himself to Moses in Exodus 3:14, saying,

I AM WHO I AM. (Exodus 3:14 NLT)

This phrase—"I AM"—is rich with meaning. It shows that God is not defined by time, circumstances, or limitations; He simply is. He has no origin and no end. He does not depend on anything or anyone. "I AM" means God is constant, complete, and unchanging. He is everything we need: always present, always faithful.

In Hebrew, the name is written with four consonants: YHWH. This is called the Tetragrammaton, and because ancient Hebrew was written without vowels, the exact pronunciation was not recorded.

Yahweh is a commonly accepted vocalization. In reverence for the holiness of this name, Jewish scribes avoided saying it aloud. Instead, they said Adonai ("Lord"), and many English Bible translations reflect this by using LORD in all capital letters wherever Yahweh appears in the original text.

WHAT DOES THIS NAME TELL US ABOUT GOD?

- **He is Eternal**: He wasn't created and will never cease to be.
- **He is Self-Sufficient**: He doesn't need anything outside of Himself to exist.
- **He is Unchanging**: His character and promises remain the same.
- **He is Personal**: Yahweh is the name He gave this name when forming a covenant relationship with His people.
- **He is Present**: "I AM" means He is with us now, not just in the past or future.

When we pray to Yahweh, we are calling on the **unchanging**, **ever-present**, **all-sufficient** God. He is everything we are not and yet everything we need.

OTHER NAMES OF GOD TO KNOW AND USE

- **El Shaddai** (God Almighty): El Shaddai speaks of God's all-sufficiency and power (Genesis 17:1).

- **Jehovah Jireh** (The Lord Will Provide): God sees your need before you even ask and makes a way (Genesis 22:14).

- **Jehovah Rapha** (The Lord Who Heals): God is the healer of bodies, minds, relationships, and hearts (Exodus 15:26).

- **Jehovah Nissi** (The Lord Is My Banner): He fights for you. He is your victory (Exodus 17:15).

- **Jehovah Shalom** (The Lord Is Peace): In chaos or fear, He is your peace (Judges 6:24).

- **El Roi** (The God Who Sees Me): You are never forgotten or invisible. God sees and cares (Genesis 16:13).

- **Abba** (Father): A deeply intimate word. He is not just powerful. He is personal (Romans 8:15).

HOW TO USE THESE NAMES IN YOUR WALK WITH GOD

- In **prayer**, speak His names. If you're in need, say, *"Jehovah Jireh, I trust You to provide."*

- In **worship**, sing or journal about His character: *"You are El Roi. You see me when I feel alone."*

- In **spiritual struggle**, declare who He is out loud as a reminder to yourself and a resistance to fear: *"Jehovah Shalom, you are my peace when fear tries to take hold."*

The names of God aren't just titles; they're invitations. Each one reveals a part of His character, offering us a way to know Him more personally. Keep calling on Him. He is who He says He is.

TAKE A MOMENT

Take time to let this settle. You don't have to fully understand it all today. Just sit with what you've read. God is patient, and He knows this might be brand new. As you move into the journal section, don't worry about saying the "right" thing. This is your space to be honest, curious, and open. Bring your full self here. God already knows you, and He loves you as you are.

JOURNAL PROMPTS

What stood out to me in what I just read?

What feels confusing?

How has my view of God changed (even slightly) since beginning this workbook?

How does it feel to know God truly knows and sees me?

What do I want to ask Him right now?

JESUS: GOD THE SON

Jesus is at the heart of the Christian faith. He is God's Son, sent to live among us to show what God's love looks like in action. Through His life, death, and resurrection, Jesus made a way for us to be close to God, no matter where we've been or what we've done.

Jesus wasn't just a good teacher or a historical figure. He is fully God and fully human, able to understand our struggles and offer us grace and hope. Learning about who Jesus is helps us understand God's incredible love for us and the gift of new life He offers to everyone who believes.

WHO HE IS

- **The Son of God**

  The Father has sent his Son to be the Savior of the world. (1 John 4:14)

- **Fully Human and Fully Divine**

  The Word became flesh and made his dwelling among us. (John 1:14)

- **The Savior and Rescuer (born of a virgin)**

  Today in the town of David a Savior has been born to you; he is the Messiah, the Lord. (Luke 2:11)

- **Our Example, Teacher, and Friend**

  I have set you an example that you should do as I have done for you. (John 13:15)

  I no longer call you servants... Instead, I have called you friends. (John 15:15)

- **God in the Flesh (sent to make a way back to Him)**

  God was pleased to have all his fullness dwell in him. (Colossians 1:19)

- **The Lamb of God**

  Behold, the Lamb of God, who takes away the sin of the world! (John 1:29)

- **The Good Shepherd (who cares for His sheep)**

  I am the good shepherd. The good shepherd lays down his life for the sheep. (John 10:11)

- **The One Who Conquered Death (and gives eternal life)**

  Jesus said to her, "I am the resurrection and the life. The one who believes in me will live, even though they die." (John 11:25)

- **The Eternal King**

He was given authority, honor, and sovereignty over all the nations of the world, so that people of every race and nation and language would obey Him. His rule is eternal—it will never end. His kingdom will never be destroyed. (Daniel 7:14)

WHAT HE HAS DONE FOR US

- **Lived a Sinless Life in a Broken World**

  He committed no sin, and no deceit was found in his mouth. (1 Peter 2:22)

- **Died on the Cross (to take the punishment for our sins)**

  He himself bore our sins in his body on the tree. (1 Peter 2:24)

- **Rose from the Dead (so we could have eternal life)**

  He is not here; he has risen! (Luke 24:6)

- **Offers Forgiveness, Freedom, and a Personal Relationship with God**

  In him we have redemption through his blood, the forgiveness of sins. (Ephesians 1:7)

- **Provides Us with Peace (that the world cannot give)**

  Peace I leave with you; my peace I give you. I do not give to you as the world gives." (John 14:27)

- **Intercedes for Us Before God the Father**

  Jesus is at the right hand of God and is also interceding for us. (Romans 8:34)

- **Gives Us the Holy Spirit (to guide and help us)**

  But the Advocate, the Holy Spirit, whom the Father will send in my name, will teach you all things. (John 14:26)

- **Offers Comfort and Hope**

  Come to me, all you who are weary and burdened, and I will give you rest. (Matthew 11:28)

- **Promises to Be with Us Always**

  And surely I am with you always, to the very end of the age. (Matthew 28:20)

- **Empowers Us to Live Changed Lives**

  Therefore, if anyone is in Christ, the new creation has come: The old has gone, the new is here! (2 Corinthians 5:17)

- **Defeated Death (so we no longer fear it)**

  But Christ has indeed been raised from the dead, the first fruits of those who have fallen asleep. (1 Corinthians 15:20)

- **Prepares a Place for Us in Eternity**

  My Father's house has many rooms... I am going there to prepare a place for you. (John 14:2)

NAMES OF JESUS TO KNOW AND USE

- **Immanuel**: God with us. Jesus came to live among us, showing that God is not distant but near (Matthew 1:23).

- **Light of the World**: Jesus illuminates the path when life feels dark, giving you clarity when you can't see ahead (John 8:12).

- **Prince of Peace**: He gives a peace the world can't give (Isaiah 9:6).

- **Bread of Life**: Just as bread sustains physical life, Jesus satisfies our spiritual needs and gives lasting life (John 6:35).

- **The Way, The Truth, and The Life**: He is the source of life and the only way to the Father (John 14:6).

- **King of Kings**: His kingdom and authority never end (Revelation 19:16).

- **Lamb of God**: Jesus was the perfect sacrifice who took away our sin and made forgiveness possible (John 1:29).

- **The Word**: Jesus is God's message made visible, revealing who God is and what He is like (John 1:1, 14).

TAKE A MOMENT

Even if you've heard about Jesus before, take a deep breath and let this part sink in: He came for you. He died knowing exactly what your life would look like, and He still chose to go to the cross. As you journal, don't hold back. Your questions, awe, and hesitations—they all belong here.

JOURNAL PROMPTS

What do I want to say to Jesus after reading this?

Do I believe He really died and rose again?

What part of His story feels the most personal to me?

THE HOLY SPIRIT: GOD WITHIN US

The Holy Spirit is not a distant power or an abstract presence. He is fully God, living within every believer. After Jesus died, rose again, and returned to the Father, He sent the Holy Spirit to dwell within us, making it possible to walk closely with God each day. He comforts, strengthens, and transforms us from the inside out. He leads us through quiet nudges and clear conviction, always in ways that align with God's Word and draw us closer to Jesus. When we feel unsure, He offers direction. When we pray, He helps us know what to say. He is not just beside us but within us, guiding and empowering us as we grow.

Think of the Holy Spirit as God's presence with us. Jesus made the way for a relationship with God, and the Holy Spirit is how we experience that relationship each day.

WHO HE IS

- **The Spirit of God**

  Now the Lord is the Spirit... (2 Corinthians 3:17)

- **Not a Force but a Person of the Trinity**

  When the Advocate comes... the Spirit of truth... he will testify about me. (John 15:26)

- **Lives Inside Believers (to guide and comfort)**

The Spirit helps us in our weakness. (Romans 8:26)

- **Intercedes for Us (when we don't know what to pray)**
  In the same way, the Spirit intercedes for God's people. (Romans 8:27)

WHAT HE DOES FOR US

- **Lives Within Us (reminding us of what Jesus taught)**
  The Holy Spirit... will teach you all things and remind you. (John 14:26)

- **Produces Fruit in Us (like love, joy, peace, and patience)**
  The fruit of the Spirit is love, joy, peace, forbearance... (Galatians 5:22–23)

- **Guides Us (in making wise decisions)**
  Teach me to do your will, for you are my God; may your good Spirit lead me on level ground. (Psalm 143:10)

- **Empowers Us (to live boldly for God)**
  But you will receive power when the Holy Spirit comes on you. (Acts 1:8)

- **Guides and Teaches Us Daily**
  When he, the Spirit of truth, comes, he will guide you into all the truth. (John 16:13)

- **Gives Spiritual Gifts (to equip and build up the church)**
  There are different kinds of gifts, but the same Spirit distributes them. (1 Corinthians 12:4)

- **Assures Us That We Belong to God**
  The Spirit you received does not make you slaves, so that you live in fear again; rather, the Spirit you received brought about your adoption to sonship. And by him we cry, "Abba, Father." (Romans 8:15)

- **Helps Us to Worship God (in spirit and truth)**
  God is spirit, and his worshipers must worship in the Spirit and in truth. (John 4:24)

NAMES OF THE HOLY SPIRIT TO KNOW AND USE

- **Counselor, Guide, and Teacher**: He instructs you, reminds you of truth, and gives all wisdom (John 14:26).

- **Comforter**: He calms the heart and strengthens you in weakness, bringing the peace of Jesus (John 15:26).

- **Spirit of Truth**: The Holy Spirit leads, convicts, directs your steps, and reveals all truth according to God's Word (John 16:13).

- **Helper**: The Holy Spirit leads, convicts, directs your steps, and reveals all truth according to God's Word (John 16:13).

- **Spirit of the Lord**: He empowers you for God's calling. (Luke 4:18)

- **Spirit of Glory**: He sustains you in trials and reveals God's presence (1 Peter 4:14).

TAKE A MOMENT

The Holy Spirit can feel mysterious or even intimidating—especially if this is your first time hearing about Him. That's okay! This is a relationship that deepens over time. As you move into the prompts, be curious. You don't have to "get it" all at once. Start with what you do know and go from there.

JOURNAL PROMPTS

Have I ever felt like the Holy Spirit nudged or reminded me of something?

What part of the Holy Spirit's role do I want to understand more?

Am I open to hearing from Him?

What's one thing I want to pray about after reading this chapter?

THE TRINITY: FATHER, SON, AND HOLY SPIRIT UNITED

The Trinity is one of the most amazing and mysterious truths about God. It means that God exists as three distinct persons (Father, Son, and Holy Spirit) but is still one God. They are each fully God, sharing the same divine nature, yet each has a unique role. It can be hard to fully understand it, but the Trinity shows us that God is relational and loving within Himself, three persons united perfectly in love and purpose.

While the Trinity can seem like a mystery, understanding it helps us grasp how God reveals Himself and relates to us personally. The Father created us and loves us deeply, Jesus the Son came to rescue us, and the Holy Spirit lives inside us to guide and strengthen us. Together, they work as one to bring us into a close, personal relationship with God. Understanding the Trinity is a foundation for growing in faith and knowing God more fully.

WHAT IT MEANS

- **There is One God, Existing in Three Persons (Father, Son, Holy Spirit)**

  Go therefore and make disciples of all nations, baptizing them in the name of the Father and of the Son and of the Holy Spirit. (Matthew 28:19)

- **Each Person of the Trinity is Fully God (not just a "part")**

  The Word [Jesus] was with God, and the Word was God. (John 1:1)

- **God is Relational by Nature (and we're invited into that relationship)**

  I will ask the Father, and he will give you another advocate to help you and be with you forever—the Spirit of truth. (John 14:16–17)

- **The Trinity Works Together in Perfect Unity (in creation, salvation, and everyday life)**

  For there are three that testify: the Spirit, the water and the blood; and the three are in agreement. (1 John 5:7-8)

TAKE A MOMENT

If the Trinity feels confusing, you're not alone. This is one of the most talked about (and misunderstood) parts of Christian belief. Don't let the mystery scare you off. It's okay to have questions or not have the right words. The Trinity reminds us that God is big enough to be complex yet personal enough to be close. God doesn't need you to understand everything perfectly; He just wants you to come closer.

JOURNAL PROMPTS

What is my first reaction to the idea of the Trinity?

Which person of the Trinity feels most familiar to me? Why?

In what ways do I want to grow in understanding God?

FINAL THOUGHTS

In this chapter, we've started getting to know God a little better—the Father, the Son, and the Holy Spirit. They are three persons but one God, working together in ways that show how much God wants to be close to us.

We've talked about God as our Creator and loving Father, Jesus as our Savior and friend, and the Holy Spirit as our helper who is always with us.

If you still have questions about the topic, reach out to a trusted friend or pastor who can walk with you on this journey.

CHAPTER TWO

ALL ABOUT THE BIBLE

If you've never opened a Bible before—or if you've tried but didn't know where to begin—you are in the right place. The Bible can feel overwhelming at first. It's long, layered, and full of names you can't pronounce and stories you've maybe never heard. That's normal. Most of us don't pick it up and instantly understand everything.

But here's what you need to know from the start: The Bible is not just a religious book—it's God's Word written for you.

It's a story (*the* story) of God's love for His people and His plan to bring us back to Him. It's not always simple, but it's alive, and it speaks into real-life moments with hope, truth, and direction.

You don't have to be a theologian to open it. You don't need to have grown up in church. You don't even have to understand it all; you just have to be willing to show up.

WHAT IS THE BIBLE?

The Bible isn't just one book—it's a collection of 66 books written by about 40 different people over thousands of years. It's divided into two main parts.

- **The Old Testament**: God's promises and His people before Jesus' birth
- **The New Testament**: Jesus' life, teachings, and the early church

Some books are history. Some are poetry, and others are letters. Some feel confusing, and that's okay. You're not expected to understand it all right away. But here's what makes the Bible different from any other book: the Bible is the living Word of God.

That doesn't mean the words change; it means they move. They speak. They reach your heart in personal, timely ways only God can orchestrate. You can read the same verse a dozen times, and on the thirteenth, it'll hit you completely differently. This is because you're in a different place, walking through different struggles, and needing different things. God knows exactly how to speak to where you are.

> For the word of God is alive and active. (Hebrews 4:12)

When you open your Bible, you're not just reading old stories; you're opening the door for God to speak directly to you—in your life and struggles with real truth and hope.

WHAT IS THE BIBLE?

You might already have a Bible at home, or maybe you're looking for one that's easier to read or better suited to how you learn. Either way, this quick guide can help. It covers both the different translations (how the original texts were put into English) and the types of Bibles you'll come across (like study Bibles, journaling Bibles, or ones with devotionals). Whether you want something simple and readable or something to dig deeper with, there's a good fit out there for you.

WHAT IS THE BIBLE?

TRANSLATION	WHAT TO KNOW
NLT (New Living Translation)	Written in easy-to-read language. Great for beginners. Very clear and conversational while still faithful to the message.
NIV (New International Version)	A great balance between clarity and staying close to the original wording. Popular in many churches. Very approachable for first-time readers.
ESV (English Standard Version)	A more formal, word-for-word style. Good if you like structure but still want it readable. Somewhat more traditional in tone.
KJV (King James Version)	Beautiful, poetic, and historical but written in 1600s English. Can be difficult to understand if you're new to the Bible.
NKJV (New King James Version)	Keeps the feel of the KJV but with updated wording. Easier to read while still holding onto some traditional language.
CSB (Christian Standard Bible)	Clear and easy to read but still sticks closely to the original meaning. It's a newer translation that's growing in popularity.

MSG (The Message)

Not a direct translation—more of a retelling in modern, everyday language. Great for big-picture understanding but best paired with another translation for deeper study.

The best translation is the one you'll *actually read*. God can speak through any of these, so don't stress about finding the "perfect" one. Find one that makes sense and invites you to keep coming back!

BIBLE TYPES

BIBLE TYPE	WHAT TO KNOW
Study Bible	Includes notes, explanations, and cross-references to help you understand context and meaning. Great for digging deeper into Scripture, even if you're new.
Journaling Bible	Has wide margins or dedicated space for writing prayers, reflections, and notes. A great option if you like to process as you read.
Devotional Bible	Includes short devotionals placed throughout the text—often daily or themed—that help connect Scripture to everyday life.
Parallel Bible	Shows multiple translations side-by-side for comparison (like NIV next to The Message). Helpful if you want to understand different perspectives of the same verse.
Compact or Pocket Bible	Smaller-sized and easy to carry. Great for travel or keeping one in your bag or car. Often doesn't include extras like study notes.
Large Print Bible	Same content but with bigger text. Easier on the eyes, so it's helpful for long reading sessions or if you prefer less strain while reading.
Children's or Teen Bible	Written and designed with younger readers in mind but honestly helpful for any age if you want a simpler, clearer way to grasp the stories.

Pick the Bible style that fits how you connect with Scripture. Whether you like room to journal, extra study notes, or something light to carry on the go, choose the format that makes you excited to open it. The right Bible is the one that helps you stay in God's Word consistently!

BIBLE STORIES I WISH SOMEONE HAD TOLD ME

If you ever felt left out or confused when someone says, *"We all know the Bible story of ___,"* this list is for you. These are some of the most well-known Bible stories that people often reference, especially in church. If you didn't grow up hearing them in Sunday school, you're not alone. This list isn't here to overwhelm you; it's just to give you a starting point.

- Creation – Genesis 1–2
- Adam and Eve – Genesis 3
- Noah's Ark – Genesis 6–9
- Abraham and Isaac – Genesis 22
- Moses and the Burning Bush – Exodus 3
- The Ten Plagues of Egypt – Exodus 7–12
- The Parting of the Red Sea – Exodus 14
- The Ten Commandments – Exodus 20
- David and Goliath – 1 Samuel 17
- Jonah and the Big Fish – Jonah 1–4
- Daniel in the Lions' Den – Daniel 6
- The Birth of Jesus – Luke 1–2
- Jesus Feeds 5,000 – John 6:1–15
- Jesus Walks on Water – Matthew 14:22–33
- Crucifixion and Resurrection – Matthew 26–28, Mark 15–16, Luke 23–24, John 19–20
- The Prodigal Son – Luke 15:11–32
- The Good Samaritan – Luke 10:25–37
- The Early Church Begins – Acts 2

And one of my personal favorites: the story Jesus told about the shepherd who left the 99 sheep to go after the one that wandered off (Luke 15:3–7). If you've ever felt like the outsider, the newcomer, or the one who missed out, that story is for you. Jesus sees you, and He came to bring you back.

READING THROUGH THE BIBLE

TRACK WHAT YOU'VE READ, ONE BOOK AT A TIME

You don't have to read the whole Bible in a year. You don't even have to read it in order. But once you start going book by book, it can be really encouraging to see how far you've come.

Use the checklist below to mark off each book as you finish it. Every box you check is a reminder that you're showing up, learning, and letting God speak to you through His Word, even if you're doing it one chapter at a time.

OLD TESTAMENT (39 BOOKS)

☐ GENESIS	☐ EXODUS	☐ LEVITICUS
☐ NUMBERS	☐ DEUTERONOMY	☐ JOSHUA
☐ JUDGES	☐ RUTH	☐ 1 SAMUEL
☐ 2 SAMUEL	☐ 1 KINGS	☐ 2 KINGS
☐ 1 CHRONICLES	☐ 2 CHRONICLES	☐ EZRA
☐ NEHEMIAH	☐ ESTHER	☐ JOB
☐ PSALMS	☐ PROVERBS	☐ ECCLESIASTES
☐ SONG OF SOLOMON	☐ ISAIAH	☐ JEREMIAH
☐ LAMENTATIONS	☐ EZEKIEL	☐ DANIEL
☐ HOSEA	☐ JOEL	☐ AMOS
☐ OBADIAH	☐ JONAH	☐ MICAH
☐ NAHUM	☐ HABAKKUK	☐ ZEPHANIAH
☐ HAGGAI	☐ ZECHARIAH	☐ MALACHI

☐ MATTHEW   ☐ MARK   ☐ LUKE

☐ JOHN   ☐ ACTS   ☐ ROMANS

☐ 1 CORINTHIANS   ☐ 2 CORINTHIANS   ☐ GALATIANS

☐ EPHESIANS   ☐ PHILIPPIANS   ☐ COLOSSIANS

☐ 1 THESSALONIANS ☐ 2 THESSALONIANS   ☐ 1 TIMOTHY

☐ 2 TIMOTHY   ☐ TITUS   ☐ PHILEMON

☐ HEBREWS   ☐ JAMES   ☐ 1 PETER

☐ 2 PETER   ☐ 1 JOHN   ☐ 2 JOHN

☐ 3 JOHN   ☐ JUDE   ☐ REVELATION

WHERE DO I START READING?

If you're new to the Bible, starting can feel overwhelming. The good news? You don't have to read it in order, and some parts are easier and more meaningful to begin with.

Try starting with the Gospels and Acts.

The first four books of the New Testament (**Matthew, Mark, Luke, and John**) are called the **Gospels**. They tell the story of Jesus' life, teachings, death, and resurrection. Here's why they're great places to begin.

WHO WROTE THEM?

- **Matthew** was one of Jesus' disciples, a tax collector who followed Him closely.
- **Mark** wasn't one of the twelve disciples but was a close companion of Peter, one of Jesus' main followers.
- **Luke** was a doctor and historian who wasn't there in person but carefully researched Jesus' life.

- **John** was another disciple (sometimes called the beloved disciple) who had a deep, personal relationship with Jesus.

WHY DO THEY TELL SIMILAR STORIES?

Each Gospel covers many of the same events but from a different angle or emphasis. Think of it like hearing the same story told by four different friends; each one notices and highlights different details. Their perspectives and backgrounds are different, reflected in their books, which gives you a greater picture of who Jesus is.

ACTS CONTINUES THE STORY

After the Gospels, the book of **Acts** shows how Jesus' followers began spreading His message and the early church grew.

NEXT BOOKS TO EXPLORE

- **Psalm**: A collection of prayers and songs expressing every emotion: joy, sorrow, fear, and hope. Reading psalms can help you talk to God honestly, even when life feels hard.
- **Proverbs**: Short, wise sayings about living well and making good choices. It's practical and easy to understand.
- **Genesis**: This is the very first book of the Bible. It tells the story of how God created the world, the beginning of humanity, and the early stories of faith and family. It helps you understand where everything starts.
- **Romans**: Written by the apostle Paul, Romans is a letter that explains what it means to have faith in Jesus and live in God's grace. It's a foundational book about how God saves us and how we can live as new creations.
- **James**: Written by James, the brother of Jesus, this book is practical advice for everyday life. It focuses on how faith shows itself through actions, not just words. Many people love James because it's straightforward and encourages living out your beliefs in real ways.

A FEW TIPS TO GET STARTED

- Pick one book (like John or Mark) and read a chapter (or a few verses) daily.
- Write down your questions, thoughts, or anything that stands out to you.
- Don't rush. It's okay if you don't understand everything right away.
- Pray before you read, asking God to help you understand.

Starting here will help you build a foundation: meeting Jesus, learning His teachings, and getting familiar with how the Bible speaks to everyday life. From there, you'll be ready to explore more!

TAKE A MOMENT

Think about your own experience with the Bible so far. What stories or verses have stood out to you? Are there parts that feel confusing or new? Use this space to jot down your thoughts, questions, or any favorite passages you want to explore more. This is your journey—there's no rush or judgment here.

JOURNAL PROMPTS

What part of the Bible am I most curious to read first? Why?

What feelings, questions, or worries come up when I think about reading the Bible? *Excitement? Confusion? Fear? Hope?*

What do I hope to learn or experience as I read the Bible?

How can I be patient and kind to myself during this journey?

FINAL THOUGHTS

The Bible can feel big and overwhelming at first, but remember, it's a collection of stories, letters, and poems showing God's love and plan for you. You don't have to know everything right away.

Take it one step at a time, and don't be afraid to ask questions or reach out to someone you trust for help. This book is here to guide, comfort, and walk with you every step of the way.

CHAPTER THREE

WHAT DOES IT MEAN TO BE SAVED?

Starting a new life with God can feel exciting and confusing. You might hear the word "saved" often, but what does that really mean for you? Is it something you earn? How do you know if you're saved? What about baptism? Is that also part of being saved? In this chapter, we'll explore what salvation means in a clear, honest way without any pressure or judgment. This is about understanding a life-changing gift and what it looks like to take that step.

WHAT IS SALVATION?

Salvation is God rescuing you from the power of sin—the things we do that separate us from Him and cause brokenness in our lives. But here's the good news: salvation is not something you have to earn. It's a free gift from God, made possible through Jesus Christ, who died for our sins and rose again to give us new life.

When you're saved, it means your relationship with God is restored. You're starting a new journey where God walks with you—helping you grow, healing what's broken, and guiding you every step of the way. Salvation isn't just about what happens once; it's about a lifetime of change and hope through God's love.

> For the wages of sin is death, but the gift of God is eternal life
> in Christ Jesus our Lord. (Romans 6:23)

HOW DOES SALVATION HAPPEN?

Salvation comes by grace (that's God's kindness and love) through faith in Jesus. Jesus lived a perfect life, died on the cross to take the punishment for our sins, and rose again to offer us new life. When you believe in Jesus and trust in Him, you receive this gift of salvation. It's not about being perfect or having it all figured out—it's about accepting what Jesus did for you and opening your heart to Him.

> For it is by grace you have been saved, through faith—and
> this is not from yourselves, it is the gift of God—not by works,
> so that no one can boast. (Ephesians 2:8-9)

HOW DO I KNOW IF I'M SAVED?

Knowing if you are truly saved can feel uncertain at times, especially when doubts, questions, or feelings of unworthiness creep in. However, God's Word gives us clear promises and signs to trust. Below are just a few of the many ways to recognize that you have received salvation.

- **You believe in Jesus and what He did for you**: Salvation begins with faith, trusting Jesus died for your sins and rose again. It's not about being perfect but about accepting His gift.

  If you declare with your mouth, "Jesus is Lord," and believe in your heart that God raised him from the dead, you will be saved. (Romans 10:9)

- **You feel a change in your heart**: This might happen right away or grow over time. You may notice a new desire to learn more about God, to live differently, or feel a sense of peace and hope you didn't have before.

  Therefore, if anyone is in Christ, the new creation has come: The old has gone, the new is here! (2 Corinthians 5:17)

- **You want to grow in your relationship with God**: Being saved means starting a lifelong journey. You may want to pray, read the Bible, or connect with other believers—even if it feels hard or confusing at first.

  But grow in the grace and knowledge of our Lord and Savior Jesus Christ. (2 Peter 3:18)

- **You have a new hope for the future**: Salvation brings a promise of eternal life with God, no matter what happens in this life. This hope provides comfort amid struggles.

  And this is the testimony: God has given us eternal life, and this life is in his Son. (1 John 5:11)

WHY SHOULD I BE SAVED?

There are many good reasons for why salvation matters. For one, it means that one day we will be with God forever in heaven, and that's an incredible hope. But more importantly, salvation is about having a real, personal relationship with God right now. It's a relationship full of love, guidance, and peace.

Beyond those blessings, it's important to understand God is perfectly good and just. Because He is holy, He cannot ignore or be near sin (the wrong things we do that hurt ourselves and others). Justice means sin must be paid for, and that payment is serious. Without a way to be forgiven, the punishment for sin separates us from God forever. This is where Jesus comes in. God loves us so much that He sent Jesus to take the punishment we deserve. Jesus lived a perfect life, died on the cross, and rose again so that anyone who trusts in Him won't have to face that punishment. Instead, we receive forgiveness and the promise of eternal life with God.

In other words, salvation is both a rescue and a gift: Jesus took the consequences of our sin so we don't have to. That's why choosing to be saved is the most important decision we can make. It changes everything about where we're heading and how we live today.

HOW DO I RECEIVE SALVATION TODAY?

Receiving salvation is all about trusting in what Jesus has already done for you. It's not about being perfect or earning God's love; it's about believing Jesus died for your sins and rose again so you can have a restored relationship with God. If you haven't already received salvation and would like to do that today, here are a few simple steps to take:

1. **Admit** that you've sinned and have done things that separate you from God.
2. **Believe** that Jesus died and rose again to take the punishment for your sins.
3. **Choose** to trust Jesus as your Savior and Lord, inviting Him to guide your life from this moment forward.

When you do this, God promises to forgive your sins and give you a new life. If you want to receive this gift today, you can pray a prayer like this:

> Dear God, I know I have sinned and need your forgiveness. I believe that Jesus died on the cross for my sins and rose again. Please forgive me, come into my life, and help me to follow You. Thank You for loving me and giving me eternal life. Amen.

You can pray this prayer in your own words too! What matters most is that it comes from your heart. If you prayed this or want to talk more about salvation, consider reaching out to someone who can help you grow in your new journey of faith, like a trusted friend or pastor.

TAKE A MOMENT

If you just prayed to receive salvation, I want you to know how proud I am of you and how excited I am for this amazing journey you're about to go on! This is the most important decision you could ever make, and heaven is celebrating with you. You're not expected to have it all figured out right now. Just keep showing up, one step at a time, and let God guide you.

If you've been saved for a while, take a moment to reflect on that gift. Remember where He has brought you from, letting it stir up gratitude and fresh joy in your heart.

If you were saved as a child but feel like you've wandered or grown distant, know that it's never too late to rededicate your life to God. He isn't mad at you; He's waiting with open and loving arms.

JOURNAL PROMPTS

What does being "saved" mean to me today?

Do I have any fears or questions about it?

Have I ever prayed to accept Jesus? What was that like? Or what is holding me back from doing so?

What do I hope my relationship with God will look like going forward?

BAPTISM: WHAT IS IT, AND WHY DOES IT MATTER?

Baptism is an important step many believers choose to take after deciding to follow Jesus. It's a special act that shows others (and reminds you) that your life is changed.

WHAT BAPTISM REPRESENTS

- **Being Washed Clean**: Baptism symbolizes how Jesus cleanses us from our sins. Just as water washes dirt off, baptism shows how God's forgiveness makes us new inside.
- **New Life**: When you go under the water (or have water sprinkled), it represents dying to your old life and rising to live with Jesus. It's a fresh start!
- **Public Declaration**: Baptism is a way to tell your friends, family, and church that you've chosen to follow Jesus. It's an outward sign of what God is doing inside you.

> We were therefore buried with him through baptism into death in order that, just as Christ was raised from the dead... we too may live a new life. (Romans 6:4)

DOES BAPTISM SAVE ME?

It's important to know that baptism itself is **not** salvation. Salvation comes through faith in Jesus alone, not by **any** action we take. Baptism is a step of obedience and a beautiful symbol of your faith.

> Peter replied, "Repent and be baptized, every one of you, in the name of Jesus Christ for the forgiveness of your sins." (Acts 2:38)

DIFFERENT WAYS TO BE BAPTIZED

Churches may practice baptism in slightly different ways. Below are a couple of ways.

- Some fully immerse you underwater, showing the "death and resurrection" of your old life and new life.
- Others pour or sprinkle water over you as a symbol of cleansing and new birth.

No matter the method, the meaning is the same: a sign of your commitment to Jesus.

WHEN SHOULD I BE BAPTIZED?

After you decide to follow Jesus, baptism is usually the next step. It's a way of celebrating your new faith and obedience. If you haven't been baptized yet, talk to your pastor or a trusted believer about how to take this step when you're ready.

If you were baptized as a child but didn't fully understand the decision or want to do it as a personal expression of your faith, it's okay to be baptized again. Baptism as an adult isn't about erasing what was done before; it's about publicly choosing Jesus for yourself now that you understand what it means. This is a powerful act that declares your faith is real and personal.

JOURNAL PROMPTS

What does baptism mean to me personally?

How do I feel about publicly sharing my faith?

Are there any fears or questions I have about baptism?

FINAL THOUGHTS

Salvation is the beginning of everything. It's not about perfection or religion; it's knowing you're loved by a God who made a way for you to be close to Him. Baptism is your outward yes to that gift—a public declaration that your old life is gone and a new life in Christ has begun.

Whether you just made the decision or you're coming back with a new fire in your heart, know this: God isn't finished with you. He's just getting started. Keep walking, asking questions, and showing up. He'll meet you every step of the way.

PRAYER AND BUILDING YOUR RELATIONSHIP WITH GOD

Prayer doesn't require perfect words. You don't need to speak a certain way, use formal language, or have everything figured out before you talk to God. You can come to Him confused, emotional, thankful, frustrated, or unsure. Speak honestly from wherever you are, or sit quietly and simply be with Him. This chapter will help you understand what prayer is, how it can become part of your everyday life, and how it strengthens your relationship with God.

WHAT IS PRAYER?

At its simplest, prayer is talking to God. That's it. It's a conversation, not a script or a performance. Prayer is how you grow closer to God. It helps build trust, connection, and peace. Even if it feels one-sided, God is listening. It can look like:

- Saying thank you, praising Him for all the wonderful blessings in your life
- Asking for help
- Being honest about what you're struggling with
- Admitting that you don't know what to say

WHAT IF I DON'T KNOW WHAT TO SAY?

Good news: God already knows what's on your heart. He's not waiting for a perfectly worded sentence, just your honesty. You can whisper, write, think, or cry it out. There is no wrong way to begin. Try starting with something simple.

> "God, I don't really know how to do this, but I want to learn."

> "I'm overwhelmed. I don't even know what to pray for."

> "Thank You for letting me start fresh today."

> "Please help me see You today."

> "I'm struggling to believe You're really there."

WHAT DOES THE BIBLE SAY ABOUT PRAYER?

The verses below show how real and personal prayer can be and how God invites you to come to Him just as you are.

- "Then you will call on me and come and pray to me, and I will listen to you." (Jeremiah 29:12)

    What It Means: God hears you when you pray.
    Real-Life Application: When you talk to Him, He isn't ignoring you or too busy. He's listening.

- "In the same way, the Spirit helps us in our weakness. We do not know what we ought to pray for, but the Spirit himself intercedes for us through wordless groans." (Romans 8:26)

    What It Means: When you don't know what to say, the Holy Spirit steps in.
    Real-Life Application: Even when you can't put your feelings into words, God understands your heart.

- "Pray without ceasing." (1 Thessalonians 5:17 NKJV)

    What It Means: Stay connected to God throughout your day.
    Real-Life Application: Prayer doesn't have to be long or formal. Talk to God as you go—on your drive, during a break, and when you're overwhelmed.

- "Do not be anxious about anything, but in every situation, by prayer and petition, with thanksgiving, present your requests to God." (Philippians 4:6-7)

    What It Means: You can bring everything (big or small) to God in prayer.
    Real-Life Application: If you're stressed, worried, or uncertain, talk to God about it. He can bring peace that doesn't make sense in the middle of chaos.

- "The prayer of a righteous person is powerful and effective." (James 5:16)

    What It Means: Prayer works. It makes a difference, even when you don't see it right away.
    Real-Life Application: Your prayers (whether whispered or wept) matter. God is moving through them.

WHAT IF I DON'T FEEL ANYTHING?

Sometimes prayer feels powerful and intimate, like God is right there in the room with you. Other times, it can feel like your words are falling flat or bounc-

-ing off the ceiling. That can be confusing, even discouraging, but here's the truth: both experiences are normal.

Prayer isn't about getting emotional results; it's about building a relationship. Like any relationship, it takes time to build trust, familiarity, and closeness. Some days will feel full of connection, and others may feel quiet. That doesn't mean God is gone or that you're doing it wrong.

Your faith isn't measured by your feelings. God promises that He hears you whether you feel Him or not. He isn't looking for perfect words or polished prayers. He's looking for your heart, honesty, and willingness to show up.

So don't stop praying just because it feels dry. The silence isn't a sign of His absence—it may be where your faith grows the most.

God is still there. Still listening. Still loving you.

HOW CAN I MAKE PRAYER PART OF MY DAILY LIFE?

There's no set schedule or formula, but here are a few tips.

- **Start small**: One or two minutes a day is a good starting point.
- **Pair it with something you already do**: Use morning coffee, walks, commutes, or lunch breaks to help create an intentional habit.
- **Write it down**: A written prayer can feel more focused and becomes something you can look back on.
- **Be honest**: God can handle your mess!

The point isn't perfection; it's connection.

WHEN YOU DON'T KNOW WHAT TO PRAY

You don't need fancy words. You don't have to impress God. He isn't grading your grammar; He's listening to your heart. But sometimes, you just need a place to start. Below are some powerful prayers from Scripture (and a few you can adapt) for when your soul is overwhelmed, unsure, or just still learning how to talk to Him.

The Lord's Prayer: A prayer for alignment—to remind your heart who's in charge and what matters most.

> Our Father in heaven, hallowed be Your name. Your kingdom come, Your will be done, on earth as it is in heaven. Give us this

day our daily bread, and forgive us our debts, as we forgive our debtors. And do not lead us into temptation, but deliver us from the evil one. For Yours is the kingdom and the power and the glory forever. Amen. (Matthew 6:9-13 NKJV)

The Prayer of Jabez: A bold, humble prayer for God's favor, guidance, and protection.

> Oh, that You would bless me and enlarge my territory! Let Your hand be with me, and keep me from harm so that I will be free from pain. (1 Chronicles 4:10)

The "Search Me" Prayer: A prayer of repentance and surrender, asking God to gently correct and lead.

> Search me, God, and know my heart; test me and know my anxious thoughts. See if there is any offensive way in me, and lead me in the way everlasting. (Psalm 139:23-24)

The "Help My Unbelief" Prayer: A short but honest cry when faith feels fragile.

> I believe; help my unbelief! (Mark 9:24 ESV)

The Armor Prayer: A daily prayer for spiritual protection and focus.

> God, help me stand strong in Your strength. Clothe me with truth, righteousness, peace, faith, salvation, and Your Word today. Help me fight the real battle—not people but spiritual ones—and keep me alert in prayer. (Adapted from Ephesians 6:10-18)

The "Here I Am" Prayer: A simple, bold yes to whatever God asks.

> Here I am. Send me! (Isaiah 6:8)

The "Be Still" Prayer: Sometimes the prayer is just silence. Stillness. Sitting with God and letting that be enough.

> Be still, and know that I am God. (Psalm 46:10)

The "Take Every Thought Captive" Prayer: When your mind feels noisy, anxious, or overwhelmed, bring those thoughts to Jesus.

> The weapons we fight with are not the weapons of the world... We take captive every thought to make it obedient to Christ. (2 Corinthians 10:4-5)

The "Forgiveness" Prayer: When your mind feels noisy, anxious, or overwhelmed, bring those thoughts to Jesus.

> For if you forgive other people when they sin against you, your heavenly Father will also forgive you. But if you do not forgive others their sins, your Father will not forgive your sins. (Matthew 6:14-15)

The "Lay It Down" Prayer: A humble request to trade pride for wisdom and self-reliance for surrender.

> When pride comes, then comes disgrace, but with humility comes wisdom. (Proverbs 11:2)

The "Heal Me" Prayer: A cry for physical, emotional, or spiritual healing from the only One who truly restores.

> Heal me, Lord, and I will be healed; save me and I will be saved, for You are the one I praise. (Jeremiah 17:14)

A Prayer to the Holy Spirit: A request for His guidance, presence, and leadership so your steps and decisions reflect God's heart.

> Holy Spirit, fill me and lead me today. Guide my thoughts, my actions, and even my prayers. Help me to walk in step with You, responding in a way that reflects God's heart.

TAKE A MOMENT

Prayer is a conversation; it's simple, honest, and personal. Whether you're just starting out or have been praying for years, take a moment now to breathe, quiet your mind, and open your heart. There's no right or wrong way to pray—just be real with God, knowing He's ready to listen and meet you exactly where you are.

JOURNAL PROMPTS

What do I want to say to God right now?

What do I feel unsure about when it comes to prayer?

What's something I'm thankful for today?

FINAL THOUGHTS

Prayer is more than words; it's a lifeline connecting you to God. It's okay if it feels messy or quiet sometimes. What matters is that you keep showing up. Over time, you'll find that prayer becomes less about asking and more about resting in His presence. Keep the conversation going and watch how it transforms your life.

CHAPTER FIVE

THE CHURCH: COMMUNITY, BELONGING, AND WHAT TO EXPECT

When you're new to faith, walking into a church building can feel like stepping into another world. People seem to know where to go, what to do, what to say, and when to stand or sit. If you've never been part of a church before (or you've had a hard experience in the past), it's okay to feel nervous or unsure.

This chapter is here to help ease some of that tension—giving you a better idea of what "church" actually means, what you might expect, and why it can become one of the most important and comforting parts of your faith journey. The goal isn't to push you into a pew; it's to show you that **you don't have to do this alone**. (And you absolutely shouldn't do this alone.)

The church—when it's healthy and grounded in love—is a place where you can grow, be supported, ask questions, and find people who will walk alongside you. You don't have to have it all figured out to show up; just being there matters.

WHAT IS CHURCH?

A lot of people think of the church as just a building, a meeting place, or a Sunday service, but it's so much more than that. The Bible describes the church as a body: not one person or place but a community of people who believe in Jesus and are learning to follow Him together. It's both local and global, rooted in relationships, not just routines. It's not perfect (because none of us are), but it's powerful because it's built on God's love, truth, and grace.

Church is where we're reminded that we're not walking this road alone. We learn together, worship together, serve together, and carry each other's burdens when life becomes heavy. It's where we grow, even when it's messy, and where we belong, even when we feel unsure.

> Now you are the body of Christ, and each one of you is a part of it. (1 Corinthians 12:27)

> Carry each other's burdens, and in this way you will fulfill the law of Christ. (Galatians 6:2)

> Let us think of ways to motivate one another to acts of love
> and good works. And let us not neglect our meeting
> together... but encourage one another. (Hebrews 10:24-25 NLT)

At its best, church is a family—a place to grow, heal, ask questions, serve, and encounter God, not just once a week but throughout life.

WHAT SHOULD I EXPECT WHEN I VISIT A CHURCH?

If you've never been to church, it can feel like everyone else has a guidebook that you don't. The truth is, churches all do things a little differently, and that's okay.

Most services have some combination of music (worship), a message (sermon), prayer, and sometimes things like communion or announcements. You might see people raising their hands when they sing or someone being baptized. Don't worry; you're not expected to know exactly what to do. Just being there is enough. There will be kind people around to help show you the way.

Churches want people to feel welcome, especially if they're new, and you're allowed to go at your own pace.

> Therefore, accept each other just as Christ has accepted you
> so that God will be given glory. (Romans 15:7 NLT)

> Let the message of Christ dwell among you richly as you teach
> and admonish one another with all wisdom through psalms,
> hymns, and songs from the Spirit, singing to God with
> gratitude in your hearts. (Colossians 3:16)

Every church is a little different, but they all share the same goal: helping you encounter God and find community at your pace.

DIFFERENT STYLES, SAME PURPOSE

There are a lot of different kinds of churches. Some have loud music, some have choirs. Some are more formal, while others are casual. Some are part of denominations, and some are independent.

A **denomination** is a group of churches sharing similar beliefs and ways of practicing their faith. Over time, Christians have interpreted the Bible in slightly different ways, so many denominations developed (like Baptist, Methodist, and Lutheran, for example).

Think of denominations like different flavors of ice cream: the core ingredient (faith in Christ) is the same, but each has its own style. Some churches are non-denominational, meaning they aren't part of a larger group, but they still focus on teaching the Bible and following Jesus.

It's okay if you don't understand all the differences right away. What matters most isn't the name on the sign; it's what's being taught and how people are living it out. You're allowed to look for a church that feels like a good fit for you: a place where the Bible is taught, Jesus is the focus, and people are growing in love and grace.

> From him the whole body, joined and held together by every supporting ligament, grows and builds itself up in love, as each part does its work. (Ephesians 4:16)

BUT WHAT IF I'VE BEEN HURT BY CHURCH BEFORE?

Not every church experience is easy. Maybe you've been judged, ignored, or even wounded in a setting that was supposed to feel safe. That's real, and I'm sorry if that's part of your story.

The truth is churches are made up of people, and sometimes people get it wrong. But don't give up on the church because of one experience. God is still good, and healthy churches do exist. The majority of churches are full of people who genuinely care about you and your walk with God.

This isn't about forgetting what happened; it's about finding hope that there *are* places where you can heal, grow, and belong. And you don't have to rush back in. You can take your time.

> He heals the brokenhearted and binds up their wounds. (Psalm 147:3)

> May the God of hope fill you with all joy and peace as you trust in Him, so that you may overflow with hope by the power of the Holy Spirit. (Romans 15:13)

No matter where you've been, God's hope and healing are always waiting to welcome you back.

WHY DOES CHURCH MATTER?

You can know and follow Jesus on your own, but you were never meant to walk this road alone.

The early church in the Bible shared meals, prayed together, encouraged one another, and helped each other when life was hard. Church today still carries that same purpose: to give us community and strength. It's where you can learn, grow, worship, serve, and be reminded that God is still at work, even when you feel weak. It's not about showing up perfect; it's about showing up honestly.

> Two are better than one... If either of them falls down, one can help the other up. (Ecclesiastes 4:9-10)

> And they devoted themselves to the apostles' teaching and the fellowship, to the breaking of bread and the prayers. (Acts 2:42 ESV)

Church matters because it's where we find support, encouragement, and the chance to grow together in faith.

A HOSPITAL FOR SINNERS, NOT A MUSEUM FOR SAINTS

Maybe you've walked into a church and felt like you didn't belong, like everyone else had their life together. Maybe you've thought, *"I've messed up too much to be here."*

But the truth is, that's **exactly** why church exists.

Church isn't for perfect people or a museum where flawless lives are put on display. It's a hospital: a place for the hurting, struggling, and searching. Jesus said it's a place for people like you and me.

> It is not the healthy who need a doctor, but the sick. I have not come to call the righteous, but sinners. (Mark 2:17)

Even the religious leaders of Jesus' day (the ones who acted like they had it all together) were called out for missing the point. He told them:

> You are like whitewashed tombs, which look beautiful on the outside but on the inside are full of bones and everything unclean. (Matthew 23:27)

Church is where we bring our real selves (doubts, questions, and flaws) to meet a God who offers healing and grace. It's a place to grow, not perform.

You don't need to have it all figured out to show up. You just need to *come*.

WHAT DOES THIS MEAN FOR YOU?

If you've ever felt like you don't belong in church because you're not perfect, hear this clearly: **you belong here exactly as you are**.

Church is a place where you don't have to put on a mask or pretend. It's a place for healing, honest questions, support, and growing into the person God created you to be.

Church isn't a place where perfect people gather to show off how good they are; this is where imperfect people come to find healing, hope, truth, and grace.

TAKE A MOMENT

Wherever you stand with church (whether you're attending regularly, still unsure, or healing from a past experience), pause and ask God to guide your next step.

Take a few quiet minutes to talk to Him about it. You don't have to have the answers, just the openness to start the conversation.

JOURNAL PROMPTS

What are my honest thoughts or hesitations about attending a church?

What kind of church environment would help me feel at ease and open to learning?

Have I experienced pain or disappointment related to church in the past?

What would it take to let that go?

FINAL THOUGHTS

Church isn't about buildings or bulletins; it's people coming together to seek God, grow in faith, and walk through life side by side. It won't always be perfect, but it can be powerful. Don't count yourself out because you're still figuring things out. You belong in community; not once you've got it all together but right now.

CHAPTER SIX

WORSHIP AND PRAISE: MORE THAN A SONG

Let's unpack what worship and praise really mean. If you're new to faith, worship might make you think of a church band or people raising their hands during a song. While music can be a beautiful form of worship, it's only part of it.

Worship isn't just singing; it's how you live.

Praise isn't just about joy; it's a posture, even in pain.

This chapter is about learning what it means to bring your whole heart to God: in music, words, gratitude, silence, and how you live your everyday life.

Worship and praise aren't about performance; they're about presence—showing up, heart open, even when your voice is shaking or silent. Keep going. You're not doing it wrong. God sees your heart.

WHAT IS WORSHIP?

Worship is responding to who God is. It's not limited to one place, song, or moment. Worship happens when you surrender something—when you obey God even when it's hard and choose love over pride. It's when you recognize His worth and respond with your life.

> Therefore, I urge you… to offer your bodies as a living sacrifice, holy and pleasing to God—this is your true and proper worship. (Romans 12:1)

WORSHIP THROUGH MUSIC

Yes, singing is one form of worship. It is a powerful way to connect with God emotionally and spiritually. You don't have to sing well; just be honest with God. He loves to hear your voice.

Try listening to different worship songs this week. Pay attention to what lyrics speak to your heart. Write them down in the back of this workbook. Come back to them. Sing them in your car, in your kitchen, and in your quiet moments.

> Sing to the Lord, all the earth; proclaim his salvation day after day. (1 Chronicles 16:23)

WORSHIP IN THE EVERYDAY

Worship isn't confined to church or playlists. It shows up in how you treat people, respond to stress, speak, and give.

When you choose patience and forgiveness or thank God for coffee in the morning or for the strength to get out of bed, that's worship.

> So whether you eat or drink or whatever you do, do it all for the glory of God. (1 Corinthians 10:31)

WHEN WORSHIP FEELS HARD

Sometimes the last thing you want to do is worship. When you're tired, hurting, and confused, worship can feel like a stretch. But worship during the hard moments is powerful—it's not fake; it's faith. And it draws you closer to God in those tough moments.

> Even though the fig tree does not bud... yet I will rejoice in the Lord, I will be joyful in God my Savior. (Habakkuk 3:17–18)

MADE FOR MORE THAN GOING THROUGH THE MOTIONS

Worship and praise are closely connected, but they're not exactly the same. Worship is a posture of the heart: it's about surrender, reverence, and offering your life in response to who God is. Praise, on the other hand, is an expression of gratitude for what God has done. Worship often happens in the quiet, consistent places. Praise tends to rise up and overflow. Both matter, drawing us closer to God and reminding us we were made for more than just going through the motions.

WHAT IS PRAISE?

Praise is telling God (and yourself) how good He is. It focuses on God's character: His goodness, mercy, love, and strength. We praise Him not because life is perfect but because He is faithful through it all. Praise lifts our perspective and helps us remember who He is, even when we forget.

> I will bless the Lord at all times; His praise will always be on my
> lips. (Psalm 34:1 CSB)

PRAISE IS A WEAPON

When you feel overwhelmed, afraid, or under attack, praise is a powerful spiritual weapon. The Bible shows us people praising in the middle of battles, prison cells, and storms. It doesn't always change your circumstances, but it can absolutely change your heart in the middle of them.

> From the lips of children and infants you, Lord, have called
> forth your praise... to silence the foe and the avenger. (Psalm
> 8:2)

PRAISE ISN'T JUST FOR GOOD DAYS

It's easy to praise God when life is going well, but praise in the valley takes faith. That kind of praise isn't fake; it's *deep*, a declaration that God is still good even when life is not. It brings you closer to God than ever before.

> Through Jesus, therefore, let us continually offer to God a
> sacrifice of praise—the fruit of lips that openly profess his
> name. (Hebrews 13:15)

PRAISE CHANGES ATMOSPHERES AND SHIFTS OUR FOCUS

Praise lifts the room and your spirit. It invites peace, joy, and spiritual clarity, helping us stop staring at our problems and start remembering who God is. It's hard to worry about the troubles of this world when you are praising God!

> You are holy, enthroned on the praises of Israel. (Psalm 22:3
> NKJV)

> I lift my eyes to the mountains—where does my help come
> from? My help comes from the Lord, the Maker of heaven and
> earth. (Psalm 121:1–2)

TAKE A MOMENT

Pause and think about what praise looks like in your life right now. Is it a song, a whispered "thank You," a moment of stillness, or even choosing joy when it's hard?

Worship isn't only what we do on Sunday—it's how we live and respond to God's goodness, even in the messy and mundane.

JOURNAL PROMPTS

What does it mean to worship even when life is hard?

Where can I bring more worship into my everyday routine?

Write a few lines of praise to invite God into the atmosphere of your life today.

FINAL THOUGHTS

Worship isn't about performance or perfection. It's about presence—showing up, heart open, and turning your eyes to the One who never changes.

Whether you sing loud, sit quietly, lift your hands, or simply breathe deep and say, "God, You're good," your praise matters. He sees it, receives it, and meets you in it.

CHAPTER SEVEN

FAITH AND TRUST

Let's be honest... It's hard to trust someone you're still getting to know. And when it comes to God, faith and trust can feel confusing at first.

This chapter is about learning to believe even when things don't make sense. It's about taking small steps toward God, even if your knees are shaking. You don't need to "feel" strong faith to begin walking in it. Start where you are right now; that's all He asks.

WHAT IS FAITH?

Faith is believing in what you can't see and in whom you can't always explain. It's not about having everything figured out. Faith is what happens when you trust God anyway. It's choosing to believe His Word is true even when your feelings don't line up.

> Now faith is the confidence in what we hope for and assurance about what we do not see. (Hebrews 11:1)

FAITH AND FEELINGS ARE NOT THE SAME

Sometimes you won't feel like God is near, but that doesn't mean He has left you. Our feelings can be influenced by the world, our fears, and others who may not have our best interest at heart. Faith isn't the same as emotions; it holds on even when your heart feels tired or uncertain.

> We live by faith, not by sight. (2 Corinthians 5:7)

FAITH GROWS OVER TIME

You don't have to have it all figured out today. Faith grows like a muscle; the more you use it, the stronger it becomes. Start with small steps. Keep showing up and building your relationship with God. Your faith will grow in ways you didn't expect.

> The apostles said to the Lord, "Increase our faith!" (Luke 17:5)

FAITH IS FOUND IN HARD TIMES

When life hurts, trusting God doesn't always come easy, but it matters. Holding onto His promises when your heart is breaking is one of the deepest and most powerful forms of worship. You don't have to fake it; you can trust God and still ask hard questions.

> When I am afraid, I put my trust in you. (Psalm 56:3)

WHAT IS TRUST?

Trust is resting in God's character even when you don't understand His plan. It's believing He is good and faithful, not just in the easy moments but in the hard ones too. Trust doesn't require all the answers; it requires surrender.

> Trust in the Lord with all your heart and lean not on your own understanding; in all your ways submit to him, and he will make your paths straight. (Proverbs 3:5–6)

TRUST IS A DECISION, NOT A FEELING

Some days, you won't feel at peace, but that doesn't mean you're failing. Trust is choosing to anchor yourself to truth even when everything around you feels unsteady.

> You will keep in perfect peace those whose minds are steadfast, because they trust in you. (Isaiah 26:3)

TRUST GROWS IN THE WAITING

When things don't happen on your timeline, it can be tempting to take control. But trust says, "Even in the silence, even in the delay, I believe God is still working."

> The Lord is good to those whose hope is in him, to the one who seeks him. (Lamentations 3:25)

TRUST IN WHO HE IS

When you don't know what's next, remember what you do know: God is kind, near, and faithful. He sees the whole picture, and He is not finished yet.

> Those who know your name trust in you, for you, Lord, have never forsaken those who seek you. (Psalm 9:10)

TAKE A MOMENT

Where in your life do you need to loosen your grip? What have you been trying to carry on your own that you haven't fully surrendered to God? Take a deep breath and close your eyes. Tell Him what's been heavy. He's listening, He's faithful, and He's trustworthy.

JOURNAL PROMPTS

Where in my life do I struggle most to trust God right now?

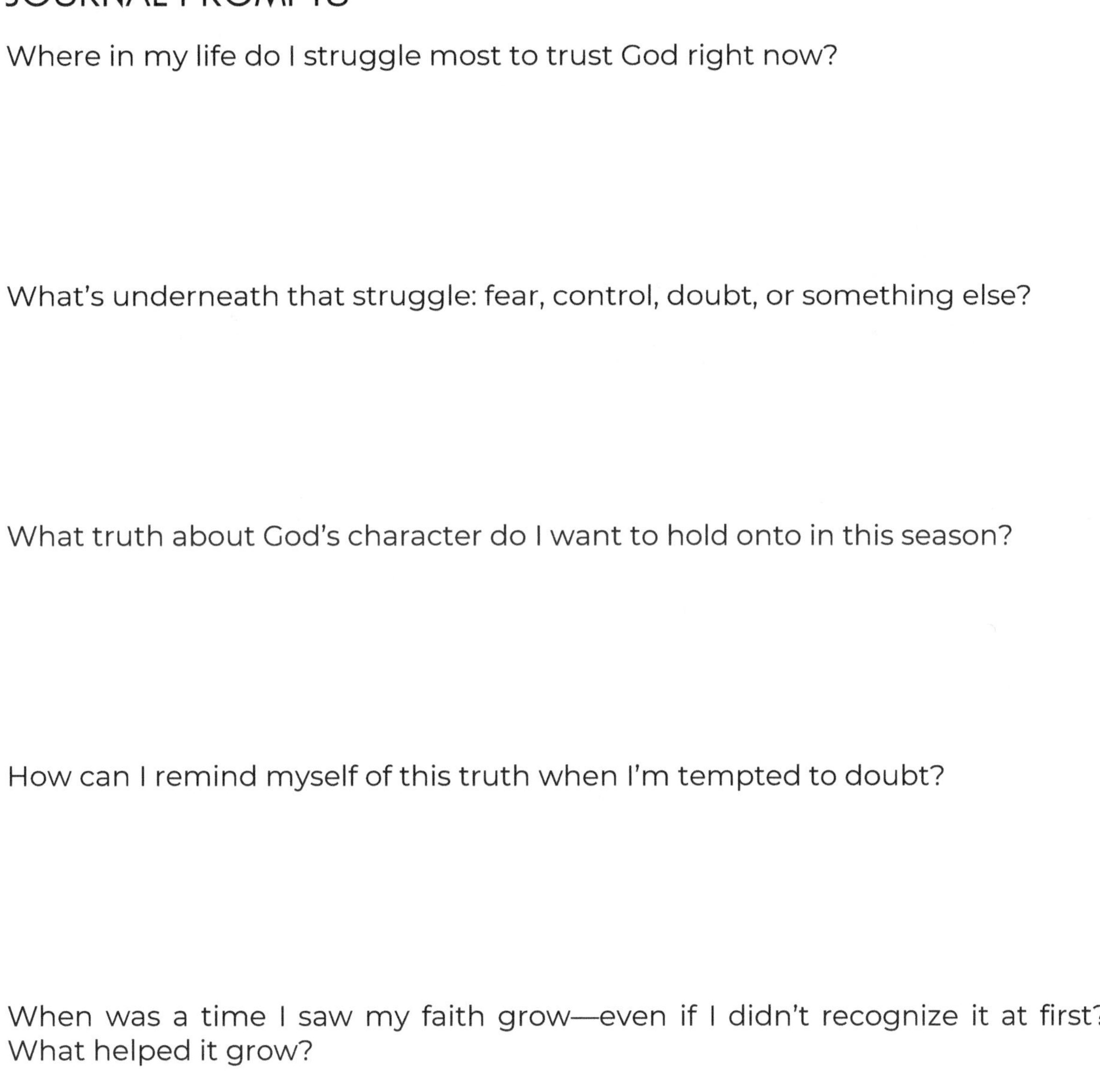

What's underneath that struggle: fear, control, doubt, or something else?

What truth about God's character do I want to hold onto in this season?

How can I remind myself of this truth when I'm tempted to doubt?

When was a time I saw my faith grow—even if I didn't recognize it at first? What helped it grow?

FINAL THOUGHTS

Faith and trust don't always look loud. Sometimes it looks like whispering "I believe You" through tears. Sometimes it looks like showing up one more day.

God never asked you to be perfect, just willing. He can do a lot with a heart that's still trying.

CHAPTER EIGHT

GRACE AND GROWTH

You're not supposed to "have it all together" right now—or ever, really.

This chapter is your reminder that your relationship with God is a journey. And like all journeys, it's filled with ups, downs, detours, and progress you don't always feel. There will be days you feel on fire for God and days you feel stuck or unsure. That's normal.

The good news? God's grace is not based on your performance. You don't earn it; you receive it.

And through that grace, you *grow*—slowly, steadily, deeply.

WHAT IS GRACE?

Grace is undeserved kindness. It's God saying, "You don't have to be perfect. I love you anyway." It's the gift that saved you and the strength that keeps you going.

> For it is by grace you have been saved, through faith—and this is not from yourselves, it is the gift of God. (Ephesians 2:8)

GRACE DOESN'T MEAN YOU'LL NEVER MESS UP AGAIN

Being saved doesn't mean you'll never sin—it means you don't have to stay stuck in it. God's grace gives you the freedom to get back up again, over and over.

> The Lord is compassionate and gracious, slow to anger, abounding in love... he does not treat us as our sins deserve. (Psalm 103:8, 10)

GRACE FUELS GROWTH

We don't grow by trying harder. We grow by staying close to Jesus. Grace doesn't let us off the hook; it calls us deeper—reminding us we *belong* to God. From that place, we *want* to grow and change.

> But grow in the grace and knowledge of our Lord and Savior
> Jesus Christ. (2 Peter 3:18)

GROWTH IS NOT LINEAR

Some days you'll feel like you're growing fast, while others you'll feel stuck. And some days might feel like you're going backward. Growth isn't a straight line; it's a process.

> Being confident of this, that he who began a good work in
> you will carry it on to completion. (Philippians 1:6)

FOCUS ON PROGRESS, NOT PERFECTION

God is not asking for perfection; He asks for surrender. Every small yes, honest prayer, and tiny step forward—it all matters.

> My grace is sufficient for you, for my power is made perfect in
> weakness. (2 Corinthians 12:9)

KEEP WALKING

There will be days when you might feel like God is distant or your efforts seem to go unnoticed. But God's timing is perfect, and your efforts are not in vain. Keep walking; the fruit will come.

> Let us not become weary in doing good, for at the proper time
> we will reap a harvest if we do not give up. (Galatians 6:9)

CELEBRATE THE SMALL WINS

Did you pray today? Open your Bible? Choose forgiveness? That's growth. God delights in every step you take toward Him, no matter how small. Don't minimize progress just because it isn't perfect.

> Do not despise these small beginnings, for the Lord rejoices to
> see the work begin. (Zechariah 4:10 NLT)

GIVE YOURSELF GRACE

This journey is new and can be scary and confusing at times. God loves you. Be sure to love yourself through this journey too. He loves you so much that He gives you more grace than you can ever imagine.

Since God is patient with you, be also patient with yourself. You don't have to earn his love or grace. He has already given it to you—receive it!

The Lord is compassionate and gracious, slow to anger, abounding in love. (Psalm 103:8)

TAKE A MOMENT

Where in your life are you expecting perfection when God is simply asking for progress? Breathe that in for a minute. His grace meets you right where you are, not where you think you *should* be. Write about those areas in the space below.

JOURNAL PROMPTS

Where have I seen evidence of God's grace in my life lately?

In what ways am I trying to earn grace instead of receiving it?

What would it look like to celebrate progress over perfection this week?

FINAL THOUGHTS

You don't have to rush your growth or earn your grace. God is patient. He's with you for the long haul. Keep showing up and saying yes. That's what growth looks like.

CHAPTER NINE

HEARING FROM GOD IN A NOISY WORLD

HOW DOES GOD SPEAK?

So… how do I know it's God and not my thoughts?

You're not alone if you've asked this. Hearing from God doesn't always mean a booming voice from heaven or a magical sign in the sky. In fact, most of the time, it's quieter than you expect—more personal and patient.

God *wants* to speak to you. He isn't hiding. But it may take time to learn how He communicates and how to tune your heart to hear Him. This chapter is here to help you slow down, pay attention, and recognize His voice in the everyday.

GOD SPEAKS THROUGH HIS WORD

The clearest and most consistent way God speaks is through Scripture. Every time you open your Bible, you're not just reading ancient words; you're giving God space to speak into your life right now.

> All Scripture is God-breathed and is useful for teaching, rebuking, correcting and training in righteousness. (2 Timothy 3:16)

GOD SPEAKS THROUGH PRAYER

Prayer isn't just talking; it's listening too. Sometimes, as you pray, you might feel a nudge, a sense of peace, or clarity you didn't have before. It might not be loud, but it's real. Give God some time during your prayers for Him to speak.

> Call to me and I will answer you and tell you great and unsearchable things you do not know. (Jeremiah 33:3)

GOD SPEAKS THROUGH PEOPLE

Sometimes God will speak through someone else: a mentor or friend, a sermon, or even a stranger. If something hits you deep and lines up with Scripture, it may be Him speaking through them.

> Plans fail for lack of counsel, but with many advisers they succeed. (Proverbs 15:22)

GOD SPEAKS THROUGH THE HOLY SPIRIT

If you've received Jesus, the Holy Spirit lives in you. He comforts, convicts, guides, and reminds you of truth. It's not always easy to explain, but it's very real. Sometimes it's a whisper, sometimes it's a deep knowing.

> But the Advocate, the Holy Spirit... will teach you all things and will remind you of everything I have said to you. (John 14:26)

GOD SPEAKS THROUGH CIRCUMSTANCES AND CREATION

God created the world, and He still uses it to point us to Him. Sometimes, He'll get your attention through a sunset, a quiet moment, dreams, music, or even a door closing on a situation you prayed about. Pay attention to what's stirring in your heart during those moments. He often speaks in the stillness.

> The heavens declare the glory of God; the skies proclaim the work of his hands. (Psalm 19:1)

The key is to test everything against Scripture. If it aligns with His truth and leads you closer to Him, He may be trying to get your attention.

GOD IS NOT THE AUTHOR OF CONFUSION

If a thought leaves you anxious, panicked, ashamed, or confused—pause. That isn't God. He speaks with clarity, peace, truth, and love, even when He corrects us.

> For God is not a God of disorder but of peace. (1 Corinthians 14:33)

GOD CAN HANDLE YOUR QUESTIONS

You don't have to pretend. If you're not sure what He's saying (or if He's saying anything at all), tell Him. Ask Him to help you recognize His voice. You don't have to have perfect spiritual hearing; just keep seeking Him.

> My sheep listen to my voice; I know them, and they follow me."
> (John 10:27)

TAKE A MOMENT

God wants to be known—He wants you to hear Him. He isn't waiting for you to "get it right" before He speaks. He is already speaking.

Sometimes it's in a whisper. Sometimes it's through a verse. Other times, it's a quiet nudge that doesn't leave you alone. You don't have to force it; you only need to slow down enough to notice.

JOURNAL PROMPTS

When was a time I felt like God was speaking to me? How did it feel? What came from this moment?

Which of the ways God speaks (Scripture, prayer, people, the Holy Spirit, etc.) feels most familiar to me right now?

Which of these areas feels the hardest to notice?

What distractions tend to drown out God's voice in my life? What would it look like to intentionally quiet those this week?

FINAL THOUGHTS

Learning to hear from God isn't about doing more; it's about making space. The more time you spend with Him, the more familiar His voice becomes. Don't rush the process. You're not failing if it takes time—you're learning and being formed.

CHAPTER TEN

TEMPTATION, SIN, AND SPIRITUAL WARFARE

One of the biggest surprises for many new believers is this: **You may feel like the fight gets harder after choosing Jesus.**

Temptation doesn't vanish the moment you put your faith in God. Sin doesn't disappear overnight. And even though your heart may be new, your habits, surroundings, and thought patterns may still feel old. You're not broken—you're in a battle, and you're not fighting alone.

WHAT IS SIN?

Sin is anything that separates us from God—in action, thought, or motive. It's falling short of who God created us to be. We often think of sin as just bad things we do, like lying, cheating, and hurting others, but it's deeper than that. Sin is also a condition of the heart. It's the brokenness we're all born into, which shows up in the way we live. That's why the Bible says we "all have sinned and fall short of the glory of God" (Romans 3:23).

But here's the truth that changes everything: Sin doesn't have to define you. God's grace is always greater. Through Jesus, both the condition and the actions of sin can be forgiven, healed, and made new.

> If we confess our sins, he is faithful and just and will forgive us our sins and purify us from all unrighteousness. (1 John 1:9)

WHAT ARE SOME EXAMPLES OF SIN?

Sin isn't only "bad behavior." It's anything that goes against God's will, whether in our actions, thoughts, or hearts. Some sins are obvious; others are more subtle. Here are just a few examples:

- Pride
- Jealousy
- Bitterness

- Unforgiveness
- Self-righteousness
- Lying or deception
- Gossip or slander
- Sexual sin (outside of God's design for marriage)
- Greed or stealing
- Substance abuse
- Holding onto idols (anything we put above God)

THE SICKNESS AND ITS SYMPTOMS

Think of sin like an illness. The condition is the sickness inside us, and the actions are the symptoms that show up on the outside. You can treat the symptoms, but the real cure must heal the root problem. That's what Jesus does. He doesn't just forgive the actions; He heals the condition of sin in our hearts.

SIN IS A STUMBLE, NOT A STOP SIGN

We all sin. What matters is how we respond. Do we hide, or do we run to God? There is grace when we repent, turn, and keep going.

> If we confess our sins, he is faithful and just and will forgive us our sins and purify us from all unrighteousness. (1 John 1:9)

THE GOAL ISN'T PERFECTION; IT'S SURRENDER

God doesn't ask you to be sinless; He asks you to be surrendered. As you walk with Him, you'll stumble less, but when you do, His grace will always meet you.

> My grace is sufficient for you, for my power is made perfect in weakness. (2 Corinthians 12:9)

Reminder: Sin is serious, but God's grace is bigger. This isn't about keeping score; it's about loving what God loves and turning away from what harms your heart, relationships, and walk with Him.

WHAT IS TEMPTATION?

Temptation is the pull toward something that goes against God's best for you. It might show up as a thought, a craving, or a pattern, but temptation itself is not sin.

Even Jesus was tempted (Matthew 4:1–11), which means feeling temptation doesn't make you weak; it means you're human.

The question is, will you dwell on it or turn from it?

> No temptation has overtaken you except what is common to mankind. And God is faithful; he will not let you be tempted beyond what you can bear. (1 Corinthians 10:13)

THERE IS AN ENEMY, BUT HE DOESN'T WIN

Spiritual struggles are real, and every believer faces them. The Bible tells us we have an enemy (Satan) who wants to pull us away from God. Thankfully, we are not alone, and God has already won the war. Jesus experienced temptation and suffering, so He knows what it feels like to struggle. Because of that, He is able to help you in your moments of weakness. Be honest about your struggles, rely on His strength, and trust that He walks with you every step of the way.

> Because he himself suffered when he was tempted, he is able to help those who are being tempted. (Hebrews 2:18)

YOU'RE NOT A BAD CHRISTIAN IF YOU STRUGGLE

There's a lie that says, "If I have doubts or hard emotions, I must be failing as a Christian." It's not true. Even people in the Bible questioned, doubted, and wrestled with God. Struggling doesn't mean you're far from God—it means you're showing up even when it's hard.

> My grace is sufficient for you, for my power is made perfect in weakness. (2 Corinthians 12:9)

WHAT IS SPIRITUAL WARFARE?

Spiritual warfare is a real part of the Christian life. It refers to the unseen battle happening every day between good and evil, truth and lies, and light and darkness. This war isn't fought with fists; it's fought with faith, truth, and prayer.

> For our struggle is not against flesh and blood, but against the rulers, against the authorities, against the powers of this dark world and against the spiritual forces of evil in the heavenly realms. (Ephesians 6:12)

THE ENEMY IS REAL BUT DEFEATED

The enemy is real and active, working to steal your peace, joy, and identity. But he is already defeated by Jesus, who came to give you abundant, eternal life that the enemy can't take away.

> The thief comes only to steal and kill and destroy; I have come that they may have life, and have it to the full. (John 10:10)

PUT ON THE ARMOR OF GOD

God equips you with everything you need to stand strong, not in your own power but in His. The armor of God protects you, grounds you in truth, and reminds you that you never fight alone.

> Put on the full armor of God, so that you can take your stand against the devil's schemes. (Ephesians 6:11)

The armor includes:

Truth (belt)

Righteousness (breastplate)

Peace (shoes)

Faith (shield)

Salvation (helmet)

God's Word (sword)

Imagine you're a soldier going into battle. You wouldn't go without armor, right? God gives us spiritual armor (truth, righteousness, peace, faith, salvation, and His Word) to protect us from spiritual attacks.

PRAYER IS A WEAPON

Now that we have put on the full armor of God, there's one more essential weapon to bring with us: prayer. While prayer isn't listed as a piece of God's armor, it is what activates and strengthens every part of it. It connects us to God, gives us discernment, and empowers us to stand firm. Without prayer, even the strongest armor is limited. But with it, we can face temptation and spiritual battles with confidence.

> And pray in the Spirit on all occasions with all kinds of prayers and requests. (Ephesians 6:18)

WORSHIP PUSHES BACK THE DARKNESS

Worship isn't just music; it's your focus. When you praise God, even in the middle of hardship, it reminds your heart who's really in charge.

> Submit yourselves, then, to God. Resist the devil, and he will flee from you." (James 4:7)

GRIEF, DISAPPOINTMENT, AND ANGER

One of the hardest parts of trusting God is learning to bring your real emotions to Him. Loss, betrayal, unanswered prayers: it's okay to grieve those things with God. He doesn't reject you in your pain; *He draws near.* You can bring Him every feeling, even the ones you've tried to hide from everyone else.

> The Lord is close to the brokenhearted and saves those who are crushed in spirit. (Psalm 34:18)

TAKE A MOMENT

Pause and reflect on where you feel most vulnerable to temptation or struggle. Remember, acknowledging those places isn't weakness. This is the first step toward standing firm. Ask God to show you how He wants to protect and strengthen you in those moments.

JOURNAL PROMPTS

What situations or feelings tend to lead me into temptation or spiritual struggle?

How have I experienced God's grace and strength in the middle of those struggles?

What part of the armor of God do I feel I need to put on more intentionally right now?

FINAL THOUGHTS

You are not alone in this battle, and victory is already won through Jesus. Your part is to keep showing up, putting on His armor, and trusting that His grace will carry you through every fight.

CHAPTER ELEVEN

SERVING AND PURPOSE

THE BIG PICTURE

One of the most beautiful things about following Jesus is that you're not just saved **from** something; you're also saved **for** something.

You were created on purpose and for a purpose. Even if you don't fully know what that looks like yet, God does. The goal of this chapter isn't to pressure you into doing something that feels too big for you to do right now. It is to help you open your heart to the idea that God wants to use your life in ways you may not even see coming.

This chapter is about discovering how serving others and following Jesus go hand-in-hand. Finding your purpose isn't about chasing a title—it's about walking in obedience.

YOU WERE MADE ON PURPOSE, FOR A PURPOSE

You weren't an accident or afterthought. God created you intentionally, with a purpose and a role in His bigger story that He prepared just for you.

> For we are God's handiwork, created in Christ Jesus to do good works, which God prepared in advance for us to do. (Ephesians 2:10)

PURPOSE DOESN'T ALWAYS FEEL BIG

Purpose isn't always flashy, and it's often found in everyday faithfulness. Even the smallest task can be sacred when it's done for God.

> And whatever you do, whether in word or deed, do it all in the name of the Lord Jesus. (Colossians 3:17)

FINDING PURPOSE STARTS WITH KNOWING GOD

You don't have to figure out your purpose all at once. Start by walking with God. He will lead you one step at a time.

Trust in the Lord with all your heart and lean not on your own understanding; in all your ways submit to him, and he will make your paths straight. (Proverbs 3:5-6)

SERVING OTHERS IS SERVING GOD

Loving others isn't just a good deed—it's an act of worship. When you serve, encourage, or care for someone in need, you honor God Himself.

Whatever you did for one of the least of these brothers and sisters of mine, you did for me. (Matthew 25:40)

Serving others can look like:

Helping your local church

Encouraging someone who's struggling

Giving your time or resources

Listening well

Praying for someone

Meeting a need, big or small

YOU DON'T NEED A STAGE TO MAKE AN IMPACT

God can use you right where you are with exactly what you have. You don't need a spotlight to make a difference, just a willing heart and your unique gifts.

Each of you should use whatever gift you have received to serve others. (1 Peter 4:10)

TAKE A MOMENT

You don't have to chase a grand calling or wait for a platform to start living with purpose.

Often, the most meaningful impact happens in the unseen moments: through kindness, faithfulness, and showing up for others with love.

JOURNAL PROMPTS

What are some gifts or skills God has given me that I may have overlooked or undervalued?

Where in my everyday life might God be calling me to serve someone else—at work, at home, or in my community?

Do I sometimes wait for "bigger" opportunities to serve?

How can I be faithful with what's in front of me today?

When have I felt most fulfilled or connected to purpose? What was I doing, and who was I serving?

What fears or doubts hold me back from stepping into purpose? What truth from Scripture can I cling to instead?

FINAL THOUGHTS

You were created on purpose and for a purpose. Keep showing up with a willing heart. God can do more through your everyday faithfulness than you can imagine.

CHAPTER TWELVE

OBEDIENCE AND REPENTANCE

WHAT IS OBEDIENCE?

Following Jesus isn't just believing; it's also responding. Obedience is how we show our love for God, and repentance is how we return when we've strayed. Both require humility and trust.

This chapter explores how turning from sin and walking in obedience brings us closer to the heart of God, not through guilt or pressure but through grace and love.

Think of it like this: God is a good Father who gives us guidance for our good. When we obey Him, we align our lives with His best for us.

Even when His instructions are difficult or go against our feelings or culture, obedience says, "I trust You more than I trust myself."

OBEDIENCE IS AN ACT OF TRUST

Obedience to God isn't following rules. It's about relationship—a response of love and trust. When we follow His lead, even in the small things, we show Him we believe He knows best.

If you love Me, you will keep My commands. (John 14:15)

Obedience can look like:

Forgiving rather than staying bitter

Serving when no one sees

Speaking truth in love

Walking away from temptation

Trusting Him with the outcome (even when

we don't understand the process)

God is looking for the posture of your heart, not perfection. A heart that wants to obey grows in obedience over time.

REPENTANCE: TURNING BACK, NOT BEATING YOURSELF UP

Repentance isn't shameful—it's about returning. To repent is to change direction, to turn away from sin, returning to God. It isn't wallowing in guilt or trying to "make it up to God."

Jesus already took care of the cost of our sin. Repentance is acknowledging our wrong, receiving His forgiveness, and allowing Him to help us walk a new way.

> Repent, then, and turn to God, so that your sins may be wiped out, that times of refreshing may come from the Lord. (Acts 3:19)

Repentance can look like:

Admitting sin without excuses

Asking for forgiveness

Receiving grace

Walking in a new direction

Returning quickly when we mess up again

Repentance is not a one-time thing. This is a rhythm in the life of every believer.

Every time we turn back to Him, He's waiting with grace, not condemnation.

WHY REPENTANCE MATTERS

Repentance opens the door to grace. It's how we draw close to God again—not in fear but with the assurance that He meets our honesty with mercy and forgiveness.

> If we confess our sins, he is faithful and just and will forgive us our sins and purify us from all unrighteousness. (1 John 1:9)

TAKE A MOMENT

Obedience and repentance are less about perfection and more about direction. God isn't expecting you to get it all right. He's inviting you to walk with Him, trust Him, and turn back quickly when you wander.

JOURNAL PROMPTS

Where is God asking me to obey, even if I don't fully understand the outcome?

Is there anything I need to turn away from that creates distance between me and God?

What does repentance look like in my daily life—not just a one-time prayer but a lifestyle of humility?

How do I typically respond when I feel convicted—do I run from God or toward Him?

FINAL THOUGHTS

Obedience isn't proving your worth to God. In it, we walk in the freedom He has already given us. Repentance isn't failure; it's a return to grace.

CHAPTER THIRTEEN

STEWARDSHIP AND TITHING

UNDERSTANDING STEWARDSHIP

We often think of money when we hear the word "stewardship," but God's call goes much deeper. Stewardship is about how we care for everything He has placed in our hands: our time, gifts, relationships, and, yes, our finances too.

Tithing is one tangible way we practice trust and obedience, returning to God what's already His. These aren't just spiritual habits; they're heart checks that keep us grounded in gratitude, humility, and purpose.

STEWARDSHIP IS ABOUT FAITHFULNESS, NOT OWNERSHIP

We don't own the resources we're given; we're entrusted with them. Whether it's our money, time, talents, or influence, God calls us to manage it all with care and purpose.

Stewardship is being faithful with what's in our hands, knowing it all ultimately belongs to Him. It is remembering that we're caretakers of His blessings, not owners of our own little kingdoms.

> Moreover, it is required of stewards that they be found faithful. (1 Corinthians 4:2 ESV)

> The earth is the Lord's, and everything in it, the world, and all who live in it. (Psalm 24:1)

STEWARDSHIP IS LIVING WITH INTENTIONAL HANDS

God doesn't ask us to have everything, only to be faithful with what we do have. Whether it's our time, talents, or resources, stewardship is about using them intentionally, not perfectly.

> Each of you should use whatever gift you have received to serve others, as faithful stewards of God's grace. (1 Peter 4:10)

Being a faithful steward might look like:

Budgeting and spending wisely

Using your gifts to serve others

Managing your time intentionally

Giving generously (not just money but

time, presence, and encouragement)

WHAT IS TITHING?

Tithing (giving the first 10% of your income back to God) is a spiritual practice rooted in trust and gratitude. It's not a tax or a "payment" to God. It is an act of worship.

> "Bring the whole tithe into the storehouse... Test Me in this," says the Lord Almighty, "and see if I will not throw open the floodgates of heaven." (Malachi 3:10)

God doesn't *need* our money, but He knows how much *we* need to be reminded that it isn't our master; *He is*. Tithing reminds us to put God first, and it fuels the work of the Church, allowing others to experience the hope we've found.

TITHING IS AN ACT OF TRUST

Tithing invites us into deeper trust, letting go of control and leaning into the belief that God will provide. It isn't about the amount but the willingness to put God first, even when it stretches us.

> Honor the Lord with your wealth, with the firstfruits of all your crops. (Proverbs 3:9)

GIVING REFLECTS THE GIVER'S HEART

Tithing isn't a religious checkbox—it's a response to God's generosity. When we give cheerfully, we align our heart with His.

> Each of you should give what you have decided in your heart to give, not reluctantly or under compulsion, for God loves a cheerful giver. (2 Corinthians 9:7)

Why it matters:

It teaches us to trust God as our Provider

It loosens money's grip on our hearts

It fuels ministry and helps people in need

It reminds us that our resources have *eternal* purpose

It shifts our mindset from scarcity to abundance

TAKE A MOMENT

Think back on how you used your time, money, and gifts in the last week. Are there places where you honored God well? Are there areas you held back or overlooked? Ask Him to show you how to steward everything He has given you with greater purpose.

JOURNAL PROMPTS

What does stewardship mean to me?

How have I seen stewardship lived out in my life?

How do I feel about tithing?

Have I experienced any heart shifts when I chose to give even when it felt uncomfortable?

What would it look like to surrender all my resources—money, time, and skills —to God for His use?

FINAL THOUGHTS

God doesn't ask for what He hasn't already given. Whether it's your paycheck, schedule, or talents, He's the source of it all. He invites you to trust Him by offering it back.

Tithing and stewardship aren't obligations—they're invitations to live open-handed and kingdom-minded.

CHAPTER FOURTEEN

SHARING THE GOSPEL AND BECOMING A DISCIPLE

At its core, the gospel is simple. We were lost, so Jesus came. He died in our place and rose again so we can have a restored relationship with God forever.

You don't need to be a theologian to share that message; you just need to *know it*, *believe it*, and be willing to open your mouth so others can hear it too.

Sharing the gospel starts with loving people, listening to their story, and being bold enough to say, "Here's what Jesus did for me."

THE GOSPEL IS THE BEST NEWS

The gospel isn't just a story; it's the truth that changes everything. Jesus came to rescue us and restore our relationship with God.

> But God shows His love for us in that while we were still sinners, Christ died for us. (Romans 5:8 ESV)

BE BOLD WITH YOUR STORY

You don't need the perfect words or a theology degree. Loving people and being honest about what Jesus has done in your life is powerful.

> Let the redeemed of the Lord tell their story. (Psalm 107:2)

WHAT IS A DISCIPLE?

A disciple is someone who responds to the call of Jesus, commits to learning His ways, and lets that relationship shape every part of their life. It's about being teachable, obedient, and rooted in His truth.

> Whoever claims to live in Him must live as Jesus did. (1 John 2:6)

A DISCIPLE FOLLOWS, NOT JUST BELIEVES

Being a disciple means surrendering daily: letting Jesus lead, teach, and shape you into His image.

> Whoever wants to be My disciple must deny themselves and take up their cross daily and follow Me. (Luke 9:23)

DISCIPLESHIP IS A DAILY DECISION

This isn't a class or a checkbox—it's time spent with God, choices made in obedience, and learning to trust Him more every day.

> If you hold to My teaching, you are really My disciples. (John 8:31)

YOU DON'T HAVE TO BE A PASTOR

Making disciples is for everyone. It looks like walking with people, praying together, and encouraging one another toward Christ.

> Go therefore and make disciples of all nations. (Matthew 28:19 NKJV)

REAL CONVERSATIONS CHANGE LIVES

You don't need all the answers. Real discipleship often looks like showing up, speaking truth in love, and walking with people.

> Always be prepared to give an answer... with gentleness and respect. (1 Peter 3:15)

TAKE A MOMENT

Think back on your own journey. Who first shared the gospel with you? Who walked with you, helping you grow?

Who can you do that for? Think of some practical steps to take to model this for that individual.

JOURNAL PROMPTS

Who helped disciple me?

What did they do that made an impact?

Who in my life needs to hear about the hope I found in Jesus?

What holds me back from sharing the gospel?

How can I live in a way that points people to Christ, not just with words but with actions?

FINAL THOUGHTS

Jesus gave us the greatest gift in the gospel and the greatest calling in discipleship. The Holy Spirit will guide you. Say yes to sharing, following, and walking with others. This is how the kingdom of God grows.

LOOKING BACK

You've reached the end of this workbook. Take a moment to pause and reflect on your journey. Return to the page titled *My Place to Start* and read what you wrote at the beginning.

Notice what feels different and what feels familiar. You may see growth in your understanding, new questions, or a greater sense of peace. There is no right way for this to look. Growth can be quiet and gradual.

Use the space below to reflect on what has shifted, what has stayed the same, and what you want to carry forward from this experience.

Some prompts to help you reflect:

- What has changed in the way I think about God?
- What feels steadier than it did before?
- What questions remain, and how do I feel about them now?
- What moments in this workbook stood out to me most?
- What do I want to remember about this part of my journey?

Thank God for what has been revealed and for what is still unfolding. Close this workbook knowing that you began something meaningful and that you are allowed to keep growing at your own pace.

____

____

____

____

____

____

____

CONCLUSION: KEEP GOING

This workbook was never meant to give you all the answers. It was meant to stir something, to help you ask better questions and spend time with God in a way that feels real.

If you made it this far, I hope you can see that God has already been at work in you. You might not see the full picture yet—you may still have doubts or feel unsure about what comes next—but your willingness to learn, open your heart, and keep showing up matters. That is the mark of someone who is truly growing!

Following Jesus does not require perfection; it requires pursuit. There will be seasons that feel steady and others that feel quiet or uncertain, but God remains faithful through them all. Keep leaning in.

I hope what you have worked through in these pages has helped you draw closer to Him, giving you space to reflect, be honest, celebrate, and grow. More than anything, may this time be a reminder that you are not alone.

God sees you. He is with you. He is for you.

Wherever this leaves you—whether you feel encouraged and ready to go deeper or still unsure of your next step—my prayer is that you keep going. Not because you feel pressure to perform, but because you have started seeing who God is and want to know Him more.

This is not the end; it is the beginning of something lasting. And I am so proud of you.

A PRAYER FROM
ME TO YOU

God,

Thank You for every person who reads these pages—for meeting them exactly where they are. I pray You continue to stir a desire in their heart to know You more, to walk in truth, and to trust You in the big and small things.

Remind them that they are never too far, insignificant, or late to be used by You. God, speak clearly, move gently, and lead them step by step as they follow You.

Give them boldness when they feel uncertain, grace when they fall, and joy that doesn't depend on their circumstances.

May they always remember they are fully known and deeply loved by You.

Amen.

LEARNING JOURNAL

WORD/PHRASE I'M LEARNING ABOUT

WHERE I HEARD IT
Was it during a sermon? In a conversation? A worship song?

WHAT I THINK IT MEANS, AND WHAT I FOUND OUT IT MEANS
Take a guess, then research or ask a mentor.

BIBLE VERSE(S) CONNECTED TO IT
Look it up or ask someone for help.

WHY THIS WORD STANDS OUT TO ME RIGHT NOW
What is God trying to show me through this?

WHAT I WANT TO ASK OR LEARN MORE ABOUT

LEARNING JOURNAL

WORD/PHRASE I'M LEARNING ABOUT

____

____

WHERE I HEARD IT

Was it during a sermon? In a conversation? A worship song?

____

____

WHAT I THINK IT MEANS, AND WHAT I FOUND OUT IT MEANS

Take a guess, then research or ask a mentor.

____

____

BIBLE VERSE(S) CONNECTED TO IT

Look it up or ask someone for help.

____

____

WHY THIS WORD STANDS OUT TO ME RIGHT NOW

What is God trying to show me through this?

____

____

WHAT I WANT TO ASK OR LEARN MORE ABOUT

____

____

LEARNING JOURNAL

WORD/PHRASE I'M LEARNING ABOUT

____

____

WHERE I HEARD IT

Was it during a sermon? In a conversation? A worship song?

____

____

WHAT I THINK IT MEANS, AND WHAT I FOUND OUT IT MEANS

Take a guess, then research or ask a mentor.

____

____

BIBLE VERSE(S) CONNECTED TO IT

Look it up or ask someone for help.

____

____

WHY THIS WORD STANDS OUT TO ME RIGHT NOW

What is God trying to show me through this?

____

____

WHAT I WANT TO ASK OR LEARN MORE ABOUT

____

____

LEARNING JOURNAL

WORD/PHRASE I'M LEARNING ABOUT

____

____

WHERE I HEARD IT

Was it during a sermon? In a conversation? A worship song?

____

____

WHAT I THINK IT MEANS, AND WHAT I FOUND OUT IT MEANS

Take a guess, then research or ask a mentor.

____

____

BIBLE VERSE(S) CONNECTED TO IT

Look it up or ask someone for help.

____

____

WHY THIS WORD STANDS OUT TO ME RIGHT NOW

What is God trying to show me through this?

____

____

WHAT I WANT TO ASK OR LEARN MORE ABOUT

____

____

LEARNING JOURNAL

WORD/PHRASE I'M LEARNING ABOUT

WHERE I HEARD IT

Was it during a sermon? In a conversation? A worship song?

WHAT I THINK IT MEANS, AND WHAT I FOUND OUT IT MEANS

Take a guess, then research or ask a mentor.

BIBLE VERSE(S) CONNECTED TO IT

Look it up or ask someone for help.

WHY THIS WORD STANDS OUT TO ME RIGHT NOW

What is God trying to show me through this?

WHAT I WANT TO ASK OR LEARN MORE ABOUT

LEARNING JOURNAL

WORD/PHRASE I'M LEARNING ABOUT

WHERE I HEARD IT
Was it during a sermon? In a conversation? A worship song?

WHAT I THINK IT MEANS, AND WHAT I FOUND OUT IT MEANS
Take a guess, then research or ask a mentor.

BIBLE VERSE(S) CONNECTED TO IT
Look it up or ask someone for help.

WHY THIS WORD STANDS OUT TO ME RIGHT NOW
What is God trying to show me through this?

WHAT I WANT TO ASK OR LEARN MORE ABOUT

LEARNING JOURNAL

WORD/PHRASE I'M LEARNING ABOUT

____

____

WHERE I HEARD IT

Was it during a sermon? In a conversation? A worship song?

____

____

WHAT I THINK IT MEANS, AND WHAT I FOUND OUT IT MEANS

Take a guess, then research or ask a mentor.

____

____

BIBLE VERSE(S) CONNECTED TO IT

Look it up or ask someone for help.

____

____

WHY THIS WORD STANDS OUT TO ME RIGHT NOW

What is God trying to show me through this?

____

____

WHAT I WANT TO ASK OR LEARN MORE ABOUT

____

____

LEARNING JOURNAL

WORD/PHRASE I'M LEARNING ABOUT

____

____

WHERE I HEARD IT

Was it during a sermon? In a conversation? A worship song?

____

____

WHAT I THINK IT MEANS, AND WHAT I FOUND OUT IT MEANS

Take a guess, then research or ask a mentor.

____

____

BIBLE VERSE(S) CONNECTED TO IT

Look it up or ask someone for help.

____

____

WHY THIS WORD STANDS OUT TO ME RIGHT NOW

What is God trying to show me through this?

____

____

WHAT I WANT TO ASK OR LEARN MORE ABOUT

____

____

LEARNING JOURNAL

WORD/PHRASE I'M LEARNING ABOUT

WHERE I HEARD IT

Was it during a sermon? In a conversation? A worship song?

WHAT I THINK IT MEANS, AND WHAT I FOUND OUT IT MEANS

Take a guess, then research or ask a mentor.

BIBLE VERSE(S) CONNECTED TO IT

Look it up or ask someone for help.

WHY THIS WORD STANDS OUT TO ME RIGHT NOW

What is God trying to show me through this?

WHAT I WANT TO ASK OR LEARN MORE ABOUT

LEARNING JOURNAL

WORD/PHRASE I'M LEARNING ABOUT

____

____

WHERE I HEARD IT

Was it during a sermon? In a conversation? A worship song?

____

____

WHAT I THINK IT MEANS, AND WHAT I FOUND OUT IT MEANS

Take a guess, then research or ask a mentor.

____

____

BIBLE VERSE(S) CONNECTED TO IT

Look it up or ask someone for help.

____

____

WHY THIS WORD STANDS OUT TO ME RIGHT NOW

What is God trying to show me through this?

____

____

WHAT I WANT TO ASK OR LEARN MORE ABOUT

____

____

PRAYER JOURNAL

WHAT'S ON MY HEART TODAY?

What am I carrying emotionally or spiritually?

____

____

WHAT AM I ASKING GOD FOR TODAY?

Prayer requests, questions, help, or guidance.

____

____

WHAT AM I PRAISING GOD FOR TODAY?

What has He done for me? What am I grateful for, even if it's small?

____

____

WHERE DID I SEE, HEAR, OR FEEL GOD THIS WEEK?

Think about moments of peace, conversations, unexpected help, or beauty.

____

____

WHAT SCRIPTURE, SONG, OR MOMENT STUCK WITH ME TODAY?

Optional: jot down anything that lifted you up or challenged you.

____

____

WHAT WILL I REMEMBER FROM TODAY'S TIME WITH GOD?

A word, feeling, truth, or reminder you don't want to forget.

____

____

PRAYER JOURNAL

WHAT'S ON MY HEART TODAY?
What am I carrying emotionally or spiritually?

WHAT AM I ASKING GOD FOR TODAY?
Prayer requests, questions, help, or guidance.

WHAT AM I PRAISING GOD FOR TODAY?
What has He done for me? What am I grateful for, even if it's small?

WHERE DID I SEE, HEAR, OR FEEL GOD THIS WEEK?
Think about moments of peace, conversations, unexpected help, or beauty.

WHAT SCRIPTURE, SONG, OR MOMENT STUCK WITH ME TODAY?
Optional: jot down anything that lifted you up or challenged you.

WHAT WILL I REMEMBER FROM TODAY'S TIME WITH GOD?
A word, feeling, truth, or reminder you don't want to forget.

PRAYER JOURNAL

WHAT'S ON MY HEART TODAY?
What am I carrying emotionally or spiritually?

____

____

WHAT AM I ASKING GOD FOR TODAY?
Prayer requests, questions, help, or guidance.

____

____

WHAT AM I PRAISING GOD FOR TODAY?
What has He done for me? What am I grateful for, even if it's small?

____

____

WHERE DID I SEE, HEAR, OR FEEL GOD THIS WEEK?
Think about moments of peace, conversations, unexpected help, or beauty.

____

____

WHAT SCRIPTURE, SONG, OR MOMENT STUCK WITH ME TODAY?
Optional: jot down anything that lifted you up or challenged you.

____

____

WHAT WILL I REMEMBER FROM TODAY'S TIME WITH GOD?
A word, feeling, truth, or reminder you don't want to forget.

____

____

PRAYER JOURNAL

WHAT'S ON MY HEART TODAY?
What am I carrying emotionally or spiritually?

WHAT AM I ASKING GOD FOR TODAY?
Prayer requests, questions, help, or guidance.

WHAT AM I PRAISING GOD FOR TODAY?
What has He done for me? What am I grateful for, even if it's small?

WHERE DID I SEE, HEAR, OR FEEL GOD THIS WEEK?
Think about moments of peace, conversations, unexpected help, or beauty.

WHAT SCRIPTURE, SONG, OR MOMENT STUCK WITH ME TODAY?
Optional: jot down anything that lifted you up or challenged you.

WHAT WILL I REMEMBER FROM TODAY'S TIME WITH GOD?
A word, feeling, truth, or reminder you don't want to forget.

PRAYER JOURNAL

WHAT'S ON MY HEART TODAY?
What am I carrying emotionally or spiritually?

WHAT AM I ASKING GOD FOR TODAY?
Prayer requests, questions, help, or guidance.

WHAT AM I PRAISING GOD FOR TODAY?
What has He done for me? What am I grateful for, even if it's small?

WHERE DID I SEE, HEAR, OR FEEL GOD THIS WEEK?
Think about moments of peace, conversations, unexpected help, or beauty.

WHAT SCRIPTURE, SONG, OR MOMENT STUCK WITH ME TODAY?
Optional: jot down anything that lifted you up or challenged you.

WHAT WILL I REMEMBER FROM TODAY'S TIME WITH GOD?
A word, feeling, truth, or reminder you don't want to forget.

PRAYER JOURNAL

WHAT'S ON MY HEART TODAY?
What am I carrying emotionally or spiritually?

____

____

WHAT AM I ASKING GOD FOR TODAY?
Prayer requests, questions, help, or guidance.

____

____

WHAT AM I PRAISING GOD FOR TODAY?
What has He done for me? What am I grateful for, even if it's small?

____

____

WHERE DID I SEE, HEAR, OR FEEL GOD THIS WEEK?
Think about moments of peace, conversations, unexpected help, or beauty.

____

____

WHAT SCRIPTURE, SONG, OR MOMENT STUCK WITH ME TODAY?
Optional: jot down anything that lifted you up or challenged you.

____

____

WHAT WILL I REMEMBER FROM TODAY'S TIME WITH GOD?
A word, feeling, truth, or reminder you don't want to forget.

____

____

PRAYER JOURNAL

WHAT'S ON MY HEART TODAY?
What am I carrying emotionally or spiritually?

____

____

WHAT AM I ASKING GOD FOR TODAY?
Prayer requests, questions, help, or guidance.

____

____

WHAT AM I PRAISING GOD FOR TODAY?
What has He done for me? What am I grateful for, even if it's small?

____

____

WHERE DID I SEE, HEAR, OR FEEL GOD THIS WEEK?
Think about moments of peace, conversations, unexpected help, or beauty.

____

____

WHAT SCRIPTURE, SONG, OR MOMENT STUCK WITH ME TODAY?
Optional: jot down anything that lifted you up or challenged you.

____

____

WHAT WILL I REMEMBER FROM TODAY'S TIME WITH GOD?
A word, feeling, truth, or reminder you don't want to forget.

____

____

PRAYER JOURNAL

WHAT'S ON MY HEART TODAY?
What am I carrying emotionally or spiritually?

____

____

WHAT AM I ASKING GOD FOR TODAY?
Prayer requests, questions, help, or guidance.

____

____

WHAT AM I PRAISING GOD FOR TODAY?
What has He done for me? What am I grateful for, even if it's small?

____

____

WHERE DID I SEE, HEAR, OR FEEL GOD THIS WEEK?
Think about moments of peace, conversations, unexpected help, or beauty.

____

____

WHAT SCRIPTURE, SONG, OR MOMENT STUCK WITH ME TODAY?
Optional: jot down anything that lifted you up or challenged you.

____

____

WHAT WILL I REMEMBER FROM TODAY'S TIME WITH GOD?
A word, feeling, truth, or reminder you don't want to forget.

____

____

PRAYER JOURNAL

WHAT'S ON MY HEART TODAY?
What am I carrying emotionally or spiritually?

WHAT AM I ASKING GOD FOR TODAY?
Prayer requests, questions, help, or guidance.

WHAT AM I PRAISING GOD FOR TODAY?
What has He done for me? What am I grateful for, even if it's small?

WHERE DID I SEE, HEAR, OR FEEL GOD THIS WEEK?
Think about moments of peace, conversations, unexpected help, or beauty.

WHAT SCRIPTURE, SONG, OR MOMENT STUCK WITH ME TODAY?
Optional: jot down anything that lifted you up or challenged you.

WHAT WILL I REMEMBER FROM TODAY'S TIME WITH GOD?
A word, feeling, truth, or reminder you don't want to forget.

PRAYER JOURNAL

WHAT'S ON MY HEART TODAY?
What am I carrying emotionally or spiritually?

____

____

WHAT AM I ASKING GOD FOR TODAY?
Prayer requests, questions, help, or guidance.

____

____

WHAT AM I PRAISING GOD FOR TODAY?
What has He done for me? What am I grateful for, even if it's small?

____

____

WHERE DID I SEE, HEAR, OR FEEL GOD THIS WEEK?
Think about moments of peace, conversations, unexpected help, or beauty.

____

____

WHAT SCRIPTURE, SONG, OR MOMENT STUCK WITH ME TODAY?
Optional: jot down anything that lifted you up or challenged you.

____

____

WHAT WILL I REMEMBER FROM TODAY'S TIME WITH GOD?
A word, feeling, truth, or reminder you don't want to forget.

____

____

GLOSSARY

ABIDE

To remain connected to Jesus in an ongoing, daily relationship.

> Remain in me, as I also remain in you... (John 15:4)

AMEN

A word meaning "so be it" or "this is true," often used to express agreement with a prayer.

> The "Amen" is spoken by us to the glory of God. (2 Corinthians 1:20)

ANOINTING

A divine empowerment from God to fulfill a specific purpose or calling.

> The Spirit of the Sovereign Lord is on me... the Lord has anointed me... (Isaiah 61:1)

ARMOR OF GOD

Spiritual protection God provides to help believers stand firm against evil and deception.

> Put on the full armor of God... (Ephesians 6:11)

ATONEMENT

Jesus taking the penalty for sin so humanity can be restored to God.

> We have now received reconciliation... (Romans 5:11)

BAPTISM

A public declaration of faith symbolizing dying to the old life and rising to new life in Christ.

> Buried with him through baptism... raised... to live a new life. (Romans 6:4)

BORN AGAIN

A spiritual rebirth that begins when a person places faith in Jesus.

> No one can see the kingdom of God unless they are born again. (John 3:3)

CALLING

God's invitation for how a believer lives, serves, and follows Him.

> Live a life worthy of the calling you have received. (Ephesians 4:1)

CHURCH

The community of believers, not just a building.

> The Lord added to their number daily those who were being saved. (Acts 2:47)

COMMUNION (THE LORD'S SUPPER)

A remembrance of Jesus' sacrifice through bread and wine (or juice).

> Do this in remembrance of me. (1 Corinthians 11:24–25)

CONDEMNATION

Guilt or shame that pushes someone away from God; believers are freed from it through Christ.

> There is now no condemnation for those who are in Christ Jesus. (Romans 8:1)

CONVICTION

A loving awareness brought by the Holy Spirit that leads to repentance and growth.

> He will prove the world to be in the wrong about sin... (John 16:8)

COVENANT

A sacred and binding promise established by God, rooted in His faithfulness.

> I have set my rainbow in the clouds... (Genesis 9:13)

CROSS

The place where Jesus was crucified, representing both sacrifice and salvation.

> The message of the cross... is the power of God. (1 Corinthians 1:18)

DAILY WALK

A phrase describing how faith is lived out in everyday life.

> What does the Lord require of you? To act justly... (Micah 6:8)

DELIVERANCE

God's act of rescuing someone from bondage or oppression.

> He has rescued us from the dominion of darkness... (Colossians 1:13)

DISCERNMENT

The ability to recognize truth, wisdom, and God's direction.

> That your love may abound more and more in knowledge... (Philippians 1:9–10)

DISCIPLE

A follower and learner of Jesus who seeks to live according to His teachings.

> Whoever wants to be my disciple must deny themselves... (Luke 9:23)

ETERNAL LIFE

Life with God that begins now and continues forever.

> Now this is eternal life: that they know you... (John 17:3)

EVANGELISM

Sharing the message of Jesus through words and actions.

> Go and make disciples of all nations... (Matthew 28:19)

FAITH

Trusting God and believing His promises even when unseen.

> Confidence in what we hope for... (Hebrews 11:1)

FELLOWSHIP

Spiritual connection and shared life among believers.

> They devoted themselves... to fellowship... (Acts 2:42)

FORGIVENESS

Releasing someone from the debt of wrongdoing.

> Forgiving each other, just as... God forgave you. (Ephesians 4:32)

FREEDOM IN CHRIST

Freedom from sin, guilt, and fear because of Jesus.

> It is for freedom that Christ has set us free. (Galatians 5:1)

FRUIT OF THE SPIRIT

Character traits produced by the Holy Spirit in a believer's life.

> Love, joy, peace, patience... (Galatians 5:22-23)

GOSPEL

The good news of Jesus' life, death, and resurrection.

> The gospel... is the power of God... (Romans 1:16)

GRACE

God's unearned love and favor.

> It is by grace you have been saved... (Ephesians 2:8)

HEART (BIBLICAL MEANING)

The center of a person's thoughts, desires, and will.

> Above all else, guard your heart... (Proverbs 4:23)

HOLY SPIRIT

God's presence living within believers to guide and empower them.

> The Holy Spirit... will teach you all things... (John 14:26)

JUSTIFICATION

Being declared righteous before God through faith in Jesus.

> Since we have been justified through faith... (Romans 5:1)

KINGDOM OF GOD

God's reign and rule, both now and in the future.

> Seek first his kingdom... (Matthew 6:33)

LAW (OLD TESTAMENT LAW)

God's commands, revealing His holiness and humanity's need for grace.

> The law was our guardian... (Galatians 3:24)

MERCY

God's compassion that withholds punishment we deserve.

> Because of the Lord's great love we are not consumed… (Lamentations 3:22–23)

NEW COVENANT

The new promise, established through Jesus' sacrifice.

> This cup is the new covenant in my blood… (Luke 22:20)

NEW CREATION

A believer's new identity in Christ.

> The new creation has come… (2 Corinthians 5:17)

OBEDIENCE

Responding to God with trust and action.

> If you love me, keep my commands. (John 14:15)

PEACE

A deep sense of rest that comes from trusting God.

> The peace of God… will guard your hearts… (Philippians 4:7)

PERSEVERANCE

Continuing to trust God through hardship.

> Blessed is the one who perseveres… (James 1:12)

PRAYER

Communicating with God through speaking and listening.

> By prayer and petition… present your requests… (Philippians 4:6)

PRIDE

Self-exaltation that places oneself above God or others.

> Pride goes before destruction… (Proverbs 16:18)

REDEMPTION

Being bought back and restored through Jesus.

In him we have redemption... (Ephesians 1:7)

RELATIONSHIP WITH GOD

A personal, ongoing connection with God made possible through Jesus.

I have called you friends... (John 15:15)

REPENTANCE

Turning away from sin and toward God.

Repent... that your sins may be wiped out. (Acts 3:19)

REST

Trusting God enough to stop striving.

Come to me... and I will give you rest. (Matthew 11:28)

REVIVAL

A renewed spiritual awakening marked by repentance and passion for God.

Will you not revive us again... (Psalm 85:6)

RIGHTEOUSNESS

Being made right with God through Jesus.

So that in him we might become the righteousness of God. (2 Corinthians 5:21)

SALVATION

Rescue from sin and death through faith in Jesus.

You will be saved. (Romans 10:9)

SANCTIFICATION

The lifelong process of being made more like Christ.

It is God's will that you should be sanctified. (1 Thessalonians 4:3)

SCRIPTURE

The inspired Word of God found in the Bible.

All Scripture is God-breathed... (2 Timothy 3:16)

SIN/SIN NATURE

Anything that separates us from God; humanity's tendency to rebel.

> For all have sinned... (Romans 3:23)

SPIRITUAL GIFTS

Abilities given by the Holy Spirit to serve others.

> There are different kinds of gifts... (1 Corinthians 12:4)

SUBMISSION

Willingly placing oneself under God's authority.

> Submit yourselves, then, to God. (James 4:7)

TEMPTATION

An invitation to act outside God's will.

> No temptation has overtaken you... (1 Corinthians 10:13)

TESTIMONY

A personal account of God's work in your life.

> By the word of their testimony... (Revelation 12:11)

TITHE

The practice of giving a portion of income to God's work.

> Bring the whole tithe into the storehouse... (Malachi 3:10)

TRANSFORMATION

The ongoing change God brings in a believer's life.

> Be transformed by the renewing of your mind. (Romans 12:2)

TRINITY

Releasing someone from the debt of wrongdoing.

> Forgiving each other, just as... God forgave you. (Ephesians 4:32)

TRUST

Relying on God's character and promises.

> Trust in the Lord with all your heart... (Proverbs 3:5–6)

WILL OF GOD

God's loving purpose and desire for humanity.

> Then you will be able to test and approve... (Romans 12:2)

WORSHIP

Honoring God through life, obedience, gratitude, and praise.

> Offer your bodies as a living sacrifice... (Romans 12:1)

MEET JESSICA

Jessica Eich came to faith as an adult and understands firsthand how disorienting those early steps of belief can feel when faith is entirely new.

As she began learning how to pray, read Scripture, and follow Jesus in everyday life, she found herself wishing for a guide who spoke plainly and honestly to those starting from scratch.

That desire eventually became *A Place to Start*.

Professionally, Jessica has spent her career in business development and relationship-focused work, experiences that shaped her heart for listening well, communicating clearly, and meeting people where they are.

Outside of work and writing, Jessica serves at her church on the photography team and in children's ministry. She enjoys traveling, reading, cooking, and spending time with her husband and family, while still continuing to discover what it means to live fully in God's presence.

Jessica is especially grateful for her husband, Chris, whose patience and love guided her as she learned to follow God.

For additional resources and to connect with Jessica personally as you take your next steps in faith, visit FlourishingTreeStudio.com.